ADEQUATELY CONSIDERED

AN AMERICAN PERSPECTIVE ON LOUIS JANSSENS'
PERSONALIST MORALS

Louvain Theological and Pastoral Monographs is a publishing venture whose purpose is to provide those involved in pastoral ministry throughout the world with studies inspired by Louvain's long tradition of theological excellence within the Roman Catholic Tradition. The volumes selected for publication in the series are expected to express some of today's finest reflection on current theology and pastoral practice.

LOUVAIN THEOLOGICAL & PASTORAL MONOGRAPHS

——————— 4 ———————

ADEQUATELY CONSIDERED

An American Perspective on Louis Janssens' Personalist Morals

DOLORES L. CHRISTIE

PEETERS PRESS.
LOUVAIN

ISBN 90-6831-211-1
D. 1990/0602/6

TABLE OF CONTENTS

ACKNOWLEDGMENTS

Without the support and expertise of many this book would have remained a spirit never incarnate. From the initial suggestion of George Worgul of Duquesne University through the encouragment and passionate dedication to excellence of David Kelly, also of Duquesne, flesh has formed on the skeleton of hope. At Leuven I received nothing but generous support in the form of time and first-hand knowledge about Janssens' method from Jan Jans, Raymond Collins, and Joseph Selling. The interview granted most graciously by Louis Janssens confirmed both my initial interest in the project and my enthusiasm for his unique contribution to Roman Catholic moral theology. My family and friends have withstood many months of only partial presence, computer burnout, and depressed rereading of imperfect text. To each of these people, who have accepted me in my limits of time and space and who have shared with me unique gifts from the treasure of their subjective cultures, I offer gratitude. Let us rejoice in this small contribution to the objective culture.

To Dick, whose enduring love quietly nourishes me and calls me to becoming.

INTRODUCTION

Roman Catholic moral theology in the late twentieth century is no longer the often predictable endeavor that it may have appeared to be in the past. Gone are the clarity and the firm answers to every moral dilemma elaborately teased from established data by a process of casuistry. As the technological knowledge of the world has expanded, and as the think-alike moral ghettos into which most people were born as late as the beginning of this century have broadened to become the global village, it is increasingly patent that the questions posed are outside the framework of past solutions and must yield to fresh approaches.

Many have struggled to find a moral methodology that is capable of meeting this challenge. In both philosophy and theology there have been attempts to find solutions to the burgeoning number of new questions. For Catholicism, especially, there is both challenge and consolation. On the one hand it is clear that the church exists as a heterogeneous population through whom the spirit speaks.[1] The words she speaks are new ones, articulating both the present and the future. On the other hand there is an abundant history of thinking that is unique to Catholicism and that deserves attention in the task of giving voice to the exciting future of moral theology.

Among those who are attempting with success to articulate this change is Louis Janssens. A man born and educated within the secure and reliable traditions of the past, Janssens is neither paralyzed by that history nor afraid to use past traditions and

---

[1] One has merely to look at the work of such contemporary Catholic thinkers as Karl Rahner to underline this reality. (See, for example, his *The Dynamic Element in the Church*.) The theology which was codified in the work of Vatican II shifted the focus in thinking in the church away from a monolithic approach to the activity of the spirit to one which recovered the reality experienced in the first century: that of the charismatic activity of the spirit not necessarily tied to an institutional framework.

insights as stepping stones to the future. At eighty Louis Janssens remains a contemporary Roman Catholic moral theologian in the fullest sense. He has retired from a lengthy career in teaching, lecturing, and writing at the Catholic University of Leuven, Belgium. His written work and influence span four decades, a world war, a national and university upheaval due to the Flemish language movement, and at least a pair of continents. One could demonstrate his impact merely by a count of the number of his students who dot the teaching faculties of outstanding universities, but his substantial contribution to contemporary moral theological method is probably even more significant. Richard Gula asserts that Louis Janssens is responsible for "one of the principal moral reflections of our times ...."[2] Janssens' work in demonstrating the difference between the moral evil resulting from conscious human choice and action and the non-moral evil (his term is ontic evil) that accompanies any human action has provided a seminal insight for contemporary Catholic moral theology. This insight has helped to free the tradition from what appears to be a constricting past by the rediscovery of its true meaning. Further, Janssens' work incarnates in ethics an existential approach compatible with such twentieth century systematic theologians as Karl Rahner.

Janssens' work has steered a course of restraint and logic in a time of challenge to the traditional Roman Catholic approach to artificial conception and birth regulation. The controversy, touched off by the Second Vatican Council and especially the encyclical *Humanae Vitae*, afforded Janssens the opportunity to reexamine the Catholic tradition in light of new knowledge. His personalist emphasis and his approach to standard Catholic method not only conserve the thinking of earlier theologians and thus remain true to the tradition, but restore it by stripping the non-essential accretions of the centuries, so that it might be reset in the context of the modern world.

While not clearly definable by an author's by-line, the ideas

[2] See Richard Gula, *What Are They Saying About Moral Norms?* (New York: Paulist, 1982) p. 69.

generated in informal dialogue in the slightly smokey leather-chaired study on the fringes of the little college town of Louvain helped to shape the thoughts of many who attended and who are known as the authors of the documents of Vatican II. Not accidentally a Who's Who of the council includes many connected with the University of Leuven and the hierarchy of Belgium.

Regrettably, Janssens' work has not had wide circulation in the United States. Much of what is known about his method, his insights, and his vast corpus has been as a result of secondary sources. Such highly visible and widely published authors as Richard McCormick and Germain Grisez, for example, have commented on his work. For a number of years McCormick's pithy annual "Notes on Moral Theology," published each March in *Theological Studies*, have analyzed and explained and critiqued Janssens' material. Grisez's commentary is often negative and reactive—his Augustine' playing opposite Janssens' Pelagius—but the frequency with which he sets up the work of Janssens in an adversarial polarity to his own thinking indicates the importance he attributes to the Belgian thinker. [3]

Janssens' students have encorporated his thinking in their own efforts. Joseph Selling, who followed his teacher as professor at the University of Leuven, has published widely, often expanding insights he gleaned as a student of Janssens. The teacher's ideas and mystique are not absent from David Kelly's survey of medical ethics in North America as well. Kelly, also a former student of Janssens, dedicated this significant work to his teacher, whose "approach to moral theology, and the sparkle in his eye, have been the inspiration for much of the thematic approach in [Kelly's book]." [4]

The lack of exposure of Janssens' work in this country is

---

[3] We shall take up Grisez's and others' critique in the latter portion of this work.

[4] David F. Kelly, *The Emergence of Roman Catholic Medical Ethics in North America: an Historical—Methodological—Bibliographical Study* (New York: Edwin Mellen Press, 1979) p. VI.

readily explained. First, much of the scholarly work of the moral theologian from Louvain remains in its original language, Dutch. While Janssens wrote some of his earlier pieces in French, the language common in Belgium's scholarly community before the upheaval of the Flemish movement and still the language spoken in some sections of the country and by many of the older citizens, the language of choice for much of his work was and is Dutch." [5] Secondly, after an initial flurry of reaction that followed the publication of his 1963 article on the limitation of conception in the *Ephemerides Theologicae Lovanienses*, [6] the nature of Janssens' contributions changed to a more, some have suggested, prudent vein. This may have slowed a discovery of his insights by the wider theological community. Certainly Rome has shown less interest in him than it has in Charles Curran, although the two scholars share some theological positions. Thirdly, Janssens' general attitude to his own work and to his notoriety is one of disinterest. While others enjoy publicity and the limelight of public recognition, Janssens prefers to think, to write, and to tend his garden away from the public. [7] If one wants to see him, he is

---

[5] Janssens' relative anonymity in this country is a distinction he shares with several other eminent thinkers whose work experienced a certain time lag in moving across the Atlantic. One thinks of Martin Heidegger, for example, or Max Scheler. Manfried Frings notes, commenting on Scheler, that he "belongs to such European thinkers whose message has remained almost unheard of in the United States..." *Max Scheler* (Pittsburgh: Duquesne University Press, 1965), p. 13. While some effort has been made to make Janssens available in this country, notably through the efforts of Raymond Collins and *Louvain Studies*, much is yet to be done.

[6] "Morale conjugale et progestogènes," *ETL* 39 (1963) 787-826. See, further Francis W. Swift, "An Analysis of the American Theological Reaction to Janssens' Stand on the Pill'," *Louvain Studies* 1 (1966-1967) 19-54. This article chronicles the publication and violent reaction to Janssens' theological advances.

[7] Richard McCormick was highly honored when Janssens elected to attend a presentation he made at Louvain. It is rare for the somewhat reclusive Janssens to attend a public event. Conversation with Richard A. McCormick, 2 April 1986, Cleveland, Ohio. This author was amused to read that Robert Kaiser, the author of more than one book on the Second Vatican Council, also had difficulty meeting with Janssens outside his home. See Robert Blair Kaiser, *The Politics of Sex and Religion* (Kansas City: Leaven Press, 1985) p. 129.

reluctantly (yet, in fairness, quite graciously) available a thirty minute walk from the Catholic University of Leuven's major bustle, behind an unused weed-covered garage, up a winding flight of stairs, in his tidy home in a picturesque residential area of Louvain. Many of those who come to the neighborhood to sightsee, however, pass by this unremarkable cottage in favor of a tour of Arenburg castle, barely five minutes beyond his door.

This present work is an attempt to remedy the omissions of the past. It proposes to set forth the methodology of Louis Janssens in itself and in its historical context.

CHAPTER ONE

PROLOGOMENA AND PERSPECTIVE

To understand the moral methodology of Louis Janssens it is necessary to become acquainted with the man himself in his context. What nourished his development and his insights? To this end we present a brief biography of Janssens, noting those under whom he studied, those with whom he associated, and those with whom he worked. Second, we explore the larger milieu of theology and philosophy that was and is present as an influence to his growth and which has served as impetus to the development of his thinking. Third, we examine the scope of Janssens' work in its chronological setting.

The Biographical Context

His Life

Louis Janssens was born in the small village of Olen, Belgium, on July 23, 1908, the son of a local farmer. His mother died when he was two. As a young boy he was not interested in learning,[1] but at the urging of the local parish priest he was persuaded to pursue an education. A speed course in French prepared the Flemish farm boy for high school in French-speaking Herentals. In 1928 he was sent to the seminary at Mechlin. He was ordained a priest on February 11, 1934, during his first year as a student in the theology faculty at the Catholic University at Louvain.

This rather ordinary beginning blossomed into an extraordi-

---

[1] This information was obtained in a personal interview with a disciple of Fr. Janssens, Jan Jans, who teaches medical ethics at the University of Leuven (31 April 1986, Louvain, Belgium). Jans left me with the impression that much of the significant work done by Fr. Janssens was begun under the urging of some superior and with some reluctance on his part.

nary academic career. In July, 1936, after the required public defense of a lengthy series of theses,[2] Janssens received his bachelor's degree in theology. He went on to graduate studies, completing a doctorate in theology the following year and his post-doctoral work[3] within the next two years. The inspiration for the latter came from Cardinal Van Roey, the archbishop of Mechlin-Brussels and primate of Belgium, who asked the promising young cleric to design a Roman Catholic response to the depersonalizing philosophies underlying the contemporaneous European political systems of the late 1930's.[4]

He began his teaching career at the seminary of St. Joseph at Mechlin the same year (1939).[5] A quirk of fate sent him to teach at Louvain as well. He replaced a professor who had been dismissed rather precipitously from the department of political and social science at the university.[6] After teaching a social philosophy course in that department, Janssens taught fundamen-

---

[2] *Program*, thesis defense of Louis Janssens, priest of the archdiocese of Mechlin, 6 July 1936, Leuven, Belgium. The custom was to have each student prepare a series of topics for discussion at a public defense. In all fourteen theses were prepared in advance. It is interesting to note the subject matter included here, especially given the areas Fr. Janssens would later pursue in his academic career. Included are such subjects as the doctrine of original sin in St. Thomas, sexual relations in marriage—with specific reference to the encyclical *Casti Connubii*, and the political philosophy of Comte.

[3] The European system differs from that in the United States. The final degree of magister is granted *after* the doctorate.

[4] Janssens notes that the book was published in too great a hurry, given its scope, and was not the best work he could have done. All the copies sold out almost immediately, however. He himself was unable to obtain a copy later for students at Leuven. This dearth was fortuitous, however, since Hitler invaded Belgium shortly thereafter. A critical Catholic response to the German corporal's political philosophy certainly would have put the author in jeopardy had it been available to read. A Dominican professor who taught with Janssens at the time quipped that the Germans were looking for the author of the book, but since there were so many people named Janssens in Belgium, they did not know which one to arrest (Interview with Louis Janssens, 29 April 1986, Louvain, Belgium.)

[5] It is interesting to compare the chronology of Janssens' career with that of Cardinal Suenens, who would play so prominent a part in Vatican II. Suenens taught at the Mechlin seminary from 1929 until he became vice rector at Catholic University of Leuven (then Louvain) in 1940. Like Janssens, his interests lay in the area of moral philosophy and with such problems as marriage.

[6] Interview with Jan Jans, 30 April 1986, Louvain, Belgium.

tal dogma in the department of systematic theology for two or three years. He then switched to the department of moral theology, where he remained until his retirement in 1978.

During his tenure at the Catholic University of Leuven Janssens taught, lectured, served as dean, wrote extensively,[7] and continued to function in the role of parish priest to those who consulted him, now the greater university community and the community at large. This "community," sometimes gathered in the comfortable black leather chairs which furnish the living room at 95 Cardinal Mercier Lane, included doctors and economists, unionists and professors, married couples and princes of the church. These associations served to nourish his thinking, shaping both the subject matter and the perspective which his theological journey would take. In dialogue the questions asked of him tended to stimulate further questions, answers, and often, modified answers, as the complexity of life challenged the traditional responses of classical theology. Joseph Selling has observed that Janssens is not a joiner, but offers advice, listens, and responds to the concerns raised by those who come to him.[8] Evidence of the esteem in which he is held is found in the tribute extended by the citizenry of Olen on the occasion of his being granted honorary citizenship.[9] Laudatory comments aptly described Louis Janssens as a "open and progressive leader ..." who was not content to remain on the fringes of things but taught about the difficult issues of modern day moral theology in such

---

[7] Much of this activity, both academic and literary, was expected of a person in Janssens' position. Everyone on the faculty of the university took his turn as department head, dean, etc. Producing articles for a variety of local Catholic papers, journals, etc., was also a part of the work. As will be evident in the list of articles published by Fr. Janssens, especially those written earlier in his career, much that was produced was in response to a local need or occasion.

[8] Interview with Joseph Selling, 7 May 1986, Louvain, Belgium.

[9] See *Lindeblad* (Spring, 1985). This local journal published the various speeches of the occasion, as well as a short biography and a list of Fr. Janssens' publications to that time. The present author has used some of the material from this journal to verify biographical data used above. See especially pp. 67-68; 34-35; 42-45.

fashion that all could understand.[10] A quick survey of his work or a poll of his students verifies this statement.

At this writing Louis Janssens continues his work. The same stamina which produced nearly two hundred books, articles, reviews, and talks, all during years of teaching, now stimulates the production of multiple stalks of asparagus (in both his front and back yards), an occasional article, as well as the early chapters of a book that will explicate fully in a single volume his personalist moral methodology.

His Associations

It is difficult to discover and to understand the major influences on a man like Louis Janssens. His adult life and work span some of the most exciting and volatile periods of the history of the Catholic church as well as of the European continent. He was born before the first world war and lived and taught through the second, in a Europe that saw first hand the physical devastation and ideological fluctuation of the times. Further, he himself is rather casual about persons who were of influence, attributing much of what he has incorporated into his method to the vast and eclectic reading and processing that have been his custom and remain so today.

His training reflected the then predictable Roman church of certain answers to time tested questions. As any Catholic who remembers those days will attest, there was clarity and security to the catechism and its format. One knew who was in charge— king, queen, pope, bishop, father, or sister—and one knew where one fit. The ferment that erupted in the wake of two world wars, and that was felt so acutely in tiny Belgium caught in the middle of the warring factions, would change that portrait forever. This was true in both the civil and the ecclesial arenas. The world of the eighties is not the world of the farmer's earnest son with the twinkle in his eye, "little Louie from Olen."[11]

[10] Ibid., pp. 34-35.
[11] In the ceremonies connected with the conferring of honorary citizenship on Fr. Janssens (see above) one of the speakers had referred to "Louis Janssens of

Among the giants of contemporary thinking whom Janssens knew or read were Martin Heidegger and members of the French personalist school. While Janssens himself denies strict parallels with some of them in his work—he claims only to have borrowed from Heiddeger the term "ontic"[12] for example—we shall see below that there are parallels to be found in the work of the two men.

Only when pressed does Janssens himself cite several people as being important to him. It is a random list, perhaps influenced by his current scholarly reading. The list includes thinkers of such diversity as Thomas Aquinas, Emmanuel Mounier, Martin Buber, and—more recently—Raymond Collins. Since much of the influence seems to have been through reading, absorption, and then incorporation into his own schema of things as his thinking developed, it is virtually impossible to demonstrate direct correlation.

The academic environment in which he worked was shared with many persons well known in the professional journals of theology. He breathed the air of Mercier and Maréchal. Both Lucien Cerfaux and Arthur Janssen witnessed his bachelor defense as professors of the university.[13] Among his contemporaries and friends were Gustave Thils, Piet Fransen, Gérard Philips, and Willem van der Marck. Among those whose work he has read are Joseph Fuchs and Bruno Schüller, Dietrich von Hildebrand and Max Scheler, Lawrence Kohlberg and Erik Erikson. While no direct connections are intended to be drawn here, it is important to understand the environment of the University of Leuven and the European continent of his time as well as the greater scholarly community up to and including the present.

His Work

The writings of Louis Janssens span an incredibly long period

Olen." Janssens himself quipped from the sidelines, "No, little Louie Janssens from Olen" (*Lindeblad*, Spring, 1985, p. 34). He is of rather short stature.

[12] Interview with Louis Janssens, 29 April 1986, Louvain, Belgium.

[13] See *Program*, p. 8.

of time. But more important than that, they span a context in history that has seen rapid change and advance in the theology of the Roman Catholic church. His earlier writings reflect an interest in the early church fathers.[14] It would be incorrect to attach too much significance to this, however, as the custom of the time was to write about the subjects that one's superiors suggested rather than to follow the bent that was necessarily one's own. The assigned magister thesis provides the first indication of his future interest in personalism. Later we shall see how this initial interest in personalism has been expanded, refined, and become the tap root for the great majority of work that Janssens has produced.

His biography shows an interest and involvement with a variety of groups, some of which occasioned the proliferation of writing in a particular vein. His interests in the fields of medicine, social justice, and marriage illustrate this idea. Some of his major acccomplishments have flowed from thinking on the sticky problems raised by those he knew. Yet in all of his work the personalist themes seeded early in his career continue to dominate. They are the constants which were to play equally well in the medical ward, the union hall, the bedroom, and in the polished halls of the council.

The Theological Journey

Even the most original thinker cannot develop in a vacuum. Aristotle stood on the shoulders of Plato, Thomas Aquinas appeared a giant because of those who preceded him. Karl Rahner's more than nine hundred articles are enhanced by the insights of Martin Heidegger. To understand Louis Janssens we must explore the philosophical and theological ground of his work.

---

[14] Janssens himself denies much significance to this early flurry of activity in the area of patristics. A cursory survey of his later work would seem to justify that conclusion.

Personalism

The theological milieu of the late thirties in Europe was permeated by personalist philosophy. This stance was to become the framework for much of Louis Janssens' work. From his first major effort after his doctoral dissertation, *Personne et société*, to the book he is currently writing, a personalist perspective dominates his thought. It is imperative, therefore, that the nature of personalism be understood.

Personalism can be traced to the ancient philosophies of Plato, Aristotle, and Plotinus.[15] At least one author has dubbed Augustine the first personalist because of his highly developed conception of the unity of mental life and the will in the human person.[16] From Boethius in the sixth century came the classical definition of person, "an individual substance of rational nature," which Thomas Aquinas later adopted.[17] Hints of personalism are found in more recent times in the works of Leibnitz, Berkeley, and Kant.

In the last century the existentialist philosophers, especially Kierkegaard, provided the fertile ground in which a modern personalism would grow, once the time was ripe and the seeds were sown. The immediate predecessor of the modern personalist movement was Rudolf Hermann Lotze, the German philosopher whose thinking would eventually influence Max Scheler through Rudolf Eucken, one of Lotze's pupils[18] Scheler's thinking, like

---

[15] Hubert Eugene Langan, "The Philosophy of Personalism and Its Educational Applications" (Ph.D. Dissertation, Catholic University of America, 1935) p. 1. Langan provides a rather succinct history of personalism in the first few pages of his dissertation.

[16] Ibid., p. 2. Here Langan quotes the work of A. C. Knudson.

[17] See Frederick C. Copleston, *Contemporary Philosophy: Studies of Logical Positivism and Existentialism,* revised edition (Westminster: The Newman Press, 1966) p. 103, for an elaboration.

[18] Langan, p. 3. Lotze saw the person as characterized by unity and uniqueness, with an aspiration toward beauty and meaning. Reality exists in the movement of the personality toward value, rather than in abstract notions. Coates sees in Lotze's critique of Hegel an anticipation of the later existentialists. See J. B. Coates, *The Crisis of the Human Person: Some Personalist Interpretations* (New York: Longmans, Green, and Company, 1949) p. 9.

that of Lotze, correlated person with value. This idea was to have a direct impact on Louis Janssens, as we shall see. The personality is the bearer of independence, creativity, and the discovery of value.[19] Scheler, along with Husserl and Heidegger, is considered to be the craftsman responsible for the foundation of contemporary European philosophy.[20] As we shall see, there is a connection with Janssens through at least one of the others as well.

In the twentieth century Charles Renouvier was the first person to designate personalism as a philosophical system. His book, *Le personalisme*, appeared in 1903. Personalism cannot be owned by any one philosopher, however. In this century it numbers among its "parents"—in addition to Scheler—Buber, Jaspers, Berdyaev, Bergson, Blondel, and Maritain.[21] Personalism has thrived wherever the situation was ripe, in a variety of contexts but generally with a similar situational impetus. Sometimes the growth has been through cross-pollination among various thinkers.

One specific form of personalism which served as the background and seedbed for Janssens is that of Emmanuel Mounier. As is the case in the ebb and flow of philosophical systems throughout history, the personalism of Mounier emerged as a reaction to the historical context of the times, in this instance the first quarter of the twentieth century.[22] The implementation of various systems of government such as Hitler's nationalist totalitarian regime in Germany, the fascist government of Italy, and

[19] Coates, p. 9.

[20] Manfried S. Frings, *Max Scheler* (Pittsburgh: Duquesne University Press, 1965) p. 21.

[21] This list is not exhaustive, however. See Emmanuel Mounier, *Personalism*, trans. Philip Mairet (Notre Dame: University of Notre Dame Press, 1952, p. VIII; and Joseph Amato, *Mounier and Maritain: a French Catholic Understanding of the Modern World*, Studies in the Humanities, 6 (University: University of Alabama Press, 1975) p. 2.

[22] Some have suggested that Mounier was not an independent or a creative thinker, but rather was representative of the era. See Coates, p. 25. For the scope of the present work, however, it is important to note the specific threads which came together to influence Louis Janssens, rather than to give a complex analysis of the philosophy of personalism. Mournier's work seems to have been influential in the development of Janssens' thinking.

the communist system in Russia, spawned a devaluation of the human person. The person became little more than a functionary within the system: a cog in a wheel where the wheel assumed all importance or value. For Mounier a reaction to this diminution of the human person began from a distance, as he saw what was happening in other countries. Later it became a lived reality in his own country of France, as Hitler moved through Europe.[23]

Europe of the 1930's and 1940's saw the breakdown of the time worn structures that had served as national bulwarks for centuries. Revolution swept Russia. Economic and political dissipation following the first world war led to the emergence of post-monarchical forms of government, whose potential to cure the protracted ills of the aging continent depended on the limitation of freedom and justice for the individuals who were a part of it. From 1932 the voice of Emmanuel Mounier, concretized in the French journal *Esprit*, became raised in France as he expounded his "philosophy of combat"[24] as a reaction to these happenings.

Mounier took great pains to identify personalism with the principle that affirms the freedom and creativity of persons while emphasizing their somewhat elusive quality. Therefore one cannot predict in advance what they will become or depend on a set world of values into which they might fit. Any radical systematization of the philosophy called personalism is thus impossible.[25] The discomfort that such a reality brings will be evident in the work of Janssens as well, especially as it coexists with a strong tendency embedded within the tradition that finds strength in conclusions rather than questions.

As a devoted Catholic, Mounier drew his ideas from its tradition, which assigned a decisive definition to person as one who finds fulfillment in transformation through freedom.[26] For Mou-

---

[23] Mounier himself was to feel the devaluation of person. He became a member of the resistance movement in France during the war and eventually was imprisoned by the Vichy government. Ironically, he was refused the sacraments by the church for his acts of civil disobedience. See Mounier, *Personalism*, p. XI.

[24] Ibid., p. IX.

[25] Ibid., p. XVI.

[26] See Mounier for expansion of these ideas. Ibid., pp. XX-XXII.

nier "the person is not an object that can be separated and inspected, but is a centre of re-orientation of the objective universe ...".[27]

In addition to Mounier, French personalism is represented by others whose work directly or indirectly had influence on Janssens. This list includes Jacques Maritain, whom some identify as a personalist and who is recognized for his impact on the philosophy of the twentieth century.

The names of Dietrich von Hildebrand and Heribert Doms dominate the theology of marriage which precedes the mid-century. Influenced by the shift to the person that was developing in philosophy these two men added a radically different approach to the theology of marriage within a Catholic context. Their approach, situated in a personalist perspective, changed the focus generally used in treating marriage—that of the *ends* of marriage and especially the end of the act of intercourse—to a perspective which concentrated on the *meaning* of marriage. In the Catholic context, if one moves from a preoccupation with the purpose (traditionally the procreation of children) to a concentration on what marriage might mean, a whole theology built from the time of Augustine onward is called into question. Hildebrand's theology, later expanded by Doms, explored the I-Thou relationship of persons that is a marriage. He saw some extrinsic goal, such as procreation, as always subordinate to this relationship and to its preservation and development.[28]

The implications of such a shift in thinking were monumental. The preoccupation with the biological aspects of the marriage act would be abandoned in favor of a genuine theology of the growth of persons in the sustained human relationship of marriage.[29]

---

[27] Ibid., p. XXVIII.

[28] See the development of the theology of these two men as treated by Theodore Mackin, *What Is Marriage?* (New York: Paulist Press, 1982) pp. 225-238.

[29] It is interesting to read the works of Hildebrand and Doms. Both men spend a considerable amount of time developing their personalist thrust in a theology of marriage. Yet when they come to dealing with the more practical approaches to the morality of marital, especially sexual activity, neither is able to

Janssens' thinking would develop in a similar vein, coming to full bloom in the season of the council. While it remains an open question whether there is a consequential or a parallel relationship between the work of Hildebrand and Doms and that of Janssens, clearly the thinking was congruent.

A discussion of personalism would be incomplete without a clarification of the types that emerged. This is particularly true in light of the criticism leveled at Janssens and others. Criticism of personalism frequently results from a misunderstanding of the philosophy and its applications. This notion will be treated in greater detail later in this work.

Bernard Häring's explication of three types of personalism is helpful in clarifying the question. He calls the first an I-oriented or humanistic personalism. This form takes each person seriously —perhaps too seriously—and has as its central goal individual self-perfection. The individual is a primary value, but a value disconnected from other values. Love of neighbor has no intrinsic value, but serves as it "heaps up merits" for the individual.[30] This form of personalism is better defined as individualism: the community or the neighbor become solely a means to the end of personal perfection. The other becomes object rather than subject. This ethical egoism is illustrated abundantly in the novels of Ayn Rand.

A second form of personalism is social personalism. Häring sees this type of personalism illustrated in the early Karl Marx, whose initial insights were a protest against an economic system which hampered human dignity. In the end his original vision was lost, however, and the person is sacrificed to the perfection of the material components of the perfect society. The best of social personalism, as described by Häring, calls for the contribution of

---

go beyond the work that was done before them. See Heribert Doms, *The Meaning of Marriage*, trans. George Sayer (New York: Sheed and Ward, 1939) and Dietrich von Hildebrand, *In Defense of Purity* (Munich: Josef Kosel and Friedrich Pustet, 1927). A sharp contrast to their approach is seen in Janssens' work which does go further, as shall be seen later.

[30] This discussion is taken from Bernard Häring, *The Christian Existentialist* (New York: New York University Press, 1968) pp. 3-10.

the talents of the individual in order to bring about social improvements for all. "In true justice and love for all, they are to effect the desired and necessary cultural, social, economic, and political renewals and improvements. Every person has a right to a standard of living that will permit him to develop his own personality."[31]

Finally Häring describes a type of personalism which he terms being-a-person in word and love. This form of personalism is a radical I-Thou personalism. The most profoundly personal experience is that which comes from an encounter with others. The human person is self-conscious as unique and worthwhile precisely because of the other persons in his or her world. It is mutual dependency rather than individualism that forms the context for personal growth. As Häring puts it, "The mutual confrontation of the Thou and the I becomes so profoundly stirring, rewarding, and enriching because persons encounter themselves in absolute uniqueness."[32] Häring sees this type of personalism reflected in the works of Buber, Scheler, Mounier, and Marcel. Personhood does not spring from within the individual as in the first type; rather it is called forth by the other. For a Christian it is called forth in the relationship with God, the "true thou before whom I am an I."[33]

Janssens' work illustrates this third type of personalism. Those who propose a negative critique of his moral methodology often mistake his type of personalism for one of the other types, as we shall see.

Existentialism

The philosophical climate of the earlier twentieth century felt the impact of existentialism in its purer form as well. The work of Husserl and Heidegger had its effect in Europe on the writing of such greats as Bultmann in scripture and Rahner in systematics.

[31] Ibid., p. 7.
[32] Ibid., p. 21.
[33] Ibid., p. 10.

Heidegger, in particular, was interested in the existential human being. His *Dasein* is always situated being, which means that one understands self only in terms of the way *Dasein* is present toward other being, that is, toward the world.[35] Human beings become themselves only in the enduring historical and temporal context of this world. Heidegger deplores the treatment of others as objects [*das Man*],[35] but insists that they, too, must be addressed as subjects. The task of human beings is to care for the world; they are "shepherd[s] of being,"[36] responsible yet not in total control.

In *Being and Time* Heidegger details the various aspects of the situated human person. Janssens' work echoes Heideggerian thought. In some cases parallels readily can be drawn, although Janssens himself denies direct connection with the German philosopher's thinking. These parallels are particularly evident in the later development of Janssens' personalism.

Neo-scholastic Revival

No discussion of the context of Janssens' work would be complete without some mention of the neo-scholastic revival. Central to this retrieval of Thomist thought in the late nineteenth and early twentieth century was the proliferation of manuals of moral theology. Originality did not follow from abundance, however. The manuals' purpose was to provide reliability and safety for Catholic thinkers.[37] Following in the wake of the modernist crisis, neo-scholasticism brought a sense of order to the philosophical arena. Quoting Gilson, a standard pre-concilar

[34] Martin Heidegger, *Being and Time*, trans. John Macquarrie and Edward Robinson (New York: Harper and Row, 1962) p. 36.

[35] Ibid., p. 164.

[36] "The Letter on Humanism," in *Martin Heidegger: Basic Writings*, ed. David Farrell Krell (New York: Macmillan Company, 1964) p. 221.

[37] The current author remembers a dog-eared introduction to philosophy text by Maritain used year after year in the Dominican Catholic college of her youth. One had only to memorize sufficiently the underlined portions—provided by previous student owners—to pass the course successfully.

college textbook comments on the intrinsic value of scholasticism:

> Now there is an excellent excuse, if not for judging what one does not sufficiently know, at least for not sufficiently knowing it.... But if any Christian master felt the same indifference with respect to the history of scholasticism, he would be less easily excusable.... This tradition is not a dead thing; it is still alive and our own times bear witness to its enduring fecundity... [T]he scholastics ... still remain for all Christian philosophers the safest guides in their quest for a rationally valid interpretation of man and the world.[38]

A strong "strict observance Thomism"[39] characterized the movement in some quarters, but this was not the only approach. Henri Bergson and his brilliant student, Jacques Maritain, sought to move scholasticism beyond its past. Maritain affirmed Thomism as a perennial philosophy, speaking to both the believer and the non-believer.[40] Especially pertinent is Maritain's stand on the human person. Drawing from his philosophical past, he made the distinction between the individual and the person. Individual constituted the material component, person the spiritual.[41] While the material component differentiates this human being from that person it is personality that allows the moving out from self to others in freedom and love.

The twentieth century revival in scholastic thinking focused on the natural law theory as an important element in moral theology. The natural law as interpreted by Aquinas, of course, is

[38] Anton C. Pegis, ed., *A Gilson Reader* (Garden City: Doubleday and Company, 1957) pp. 173-175, cited by Harry R. Klocker, S.J., *Thomism and Modern Thought* (New York: Appleton-Century-Crofts, 1962) pp. 300-301. Note here the emphasis on the safe.

[39] See Helen James John, *The Thomist Spectrum* (New York: Fordham University Press, 1966) pp. 3-15 for a discussion of this phenomenon.

[40] For further explication of Maritain's thought see Amato, especially pp. 55-76. Amato sees Maritain as anticipating the personalistic thought of Mounier. See p. 59.

[41] See John, pp.26-30; and Copelston, pp. 112-113, for further discussion. Copelston, in particular, draws parallels here among the personalists, the Thomists, and the existentialists regarding this distinction. It is not unlikely that this philosophical stew was important food for Janssens.

based on a world view that accepted a static, God-given unchangeable stance regarding the source and end of all morality.[42]
Further, the basic axiom, "do good and avoid evil," could be
extended to concrete absolute normative conclusions. These could
be applied even in such areas as biology.[43] This concept would
provide the battleground for much discussion in moral theology
in the second half of this century, especially in the area of
marriage, and would be a focal point in some of Janssens work.

The influences of neo-Thomism on Janssens' thinking sprang
from closer to home than the France of Maritain. The renewal of
Thomist thought and its harmonizing with modern scientific
discovery were furthered by persons associated with Janssens'
own university. Cardinal Mercier and his collaborators (working
roughly in the period preceding Janssens, the earliest years of the
century) were convinced that the Thomistic system of philosphy,
starting with the notion that all knowledge comes first through
the senses, was compatible with modern science, which depended
on the observation of sensate data. These philosophers saw that
philosophy must dialogue with science and integrate into its own
discipline the conclusions found there. Mercier maintained that
"scientific knowledge can be obtained only by devoting oneself to
a particular science for its own sake, and not with a view to
obtaining results which can be used in religious apologetics."[44] It
is this respect for the vast body of knowledge outside theology

---

[42] Maritain would defend the position that natural law was universal moral
law. His thesis on why not everyone accepted this idea was supported by analogy:
primitive people make mistakes about such things as the stars being holes in a
great tent. Can they not be expected to make mistakes in the perception of a
natural law? He saw an understanding and acceptance of natural law as dependent
on a "penetration by the gospel." See *The Social and Political Philosophy of
Jacques Maritain*, ed. Joseph W. Evans and Leo R. Ward (Garden City: Image
Books, 1965), pp. 43-45. Cf. Joseph Fuchs, *Natural Law: a Theological Investigation*, trans. Helmut Reckter and John A. Dowling (New York: Sheed and Ward,
1965) pp. 42-52, for example.

[43] The concept and various interpretations of the natural law will be treated in
detail in chapter four below. A selected bibliography on the subject is included
there. See p. 107, n. 43.

[44] Frederick C. Copleston, *Aquinas* (Baltimore: Penguin Books, 1955) p. 249.

that was Janssens' heritage at Louvain and which characterizes his questioning method.[45]

On the Eve of the Council

As the people of God moved into the second half of the twentieth century it became more and more clear that change was imminent. It is well known that the freedom in thinking that had developed in theology and philosophy, the strides made in liturgy, scripture, and the study of the Fathers, and the contact with systems of thought different from Roman Catholicism all found their expression and ecclesial validation on the floor of the council. Pope John's famous open windows would remain ajar for much of the twentieth century.

The initial expectation for the council was less grand. The original schemata prepared as working papers from preliminary input gathered throughout the world for the council fathers expressed nothing new, but rather repeated classic statements about the church as a perfect society, and so forth.[46] They were juridical in context and in tone, according to Cardinal Suenens' analysis.[47] The implications for Janssens' field of moral theology are clear: pre-Vatican II moral theology tended to be law oriented; that is, morally true conduct consisted in obedience to the law.

Yet John XXIII did not envision a council convened merely to reaffirm the tradition. As Robert Kaiser notes, quoting Gregory

---

[45] Closer in time to Janssens is Joseph Maréchal. One would tend to look for association between the two men. While clearly associated with the neo-scholastic revival at Louvain (the "Louvain tradition" [See John, p. 139.]), Maréchal taught at the Jesuit theology faculty rather than in the university proper. Further, his work took him more deeply into the connection between scholastic philosophy and the transcendental method, flowing from Kant, than is evident in Janssens. While the philosophical air breathed by the two teachers at Louvain was the same, there is no evidence to demonstrate dependence or connection between the two.

[46] Robert Kaiser presents some rather interesting insights into the machinations of the council. See *Inside the Council* (London: Burns and Oates, 1963) pp. 60 ff.

[47] Walter M. Abbott, *Twelve Council Fathers* (New York: Macmillan 1963) p. 35.

Baum, "John 'seemed to be smiling in two directions.' "[48] Like
the ancient god, Janus, the council promised to look not only to
the past but to the future, its second face seeking to address, as
Suenens remarked on the eve of the second session, the "dignity
of the human person, family problems, economic questions and
social justice, and the international field."[49] The joy and hope for
the modern church would be realized in the documents of the
council with a new vision and a new methodology. The progressive thinking of Louis Janssens would be a part of this horizon.

A Working Synthesis

A brief synthesis of Janssens' writings follows. No attempt will
be made to treat the material in depth at this time. Here we offer
only a chronological summary of Janssens' work. Even this is a
difficult task, since the body of his writings is substantial. In the
fifty years spanned by Janssens' scholarly career, he has produced, in addition to his magister thesis, three major books that
impact significantly on his moral methodology and several smal-
ler books, as well as over one hundred articles, some of which
contain the germ or the extension of his thinking on moral
method. His bibliography includes many occasional pieces as
well, some scholarly, some pious articles for local journals or for
a particular occasion. Within these articles can be found the
various interests and themes that dominate his work.

The magister thesis, *Personne et société* (1939), laid the foundations for his personalist methodology. It is interesting to reflect
that this work, accomplished reluctantly at the request of his
bishop, and by his admission, written in haste, should provide the
cornerstone for the major accomplishment of his life. In the two
books, *Personalisme en democratisering* (1957), and *Liberté de
conscience et liberté religieuse* (1964), and in many of his more

---

[48] Kaiser, p. 70.
[49] Abbott, p. 37.

recent articles,[50] the methodology is explicated and refined. Currently Professor Janssens is at work on a new book which will attempt to bring together into one volume the totality of his thinking on a personalist moral method.

Chronologically one can find certain themes and concentrations in the work. The earliest writings reflected the contemporaneous European interest in patristics. His first three published works were on the church fathers. Janssens denies any connection between these early efforts and later work, however.

The articles produced during the forties, the war years in Europe, are a pot-pourri on a variety of topics. Janssens, like other talented young clergy of the time, wrote on various dimensions of Christian faith for such journals—representative of the time—as *Ons Geloof* and *Onze Alma Mater*. Some of the articles he produced, however, dealt with social and political issues a daring endeavor in the throes of the Germans occupation. In the work of the forties some interesting material appears that deals with the application to moral theology of the dimensions of time and space, a theme to which he will return. Fully developed, these early insights constitute an essential part of Janssens' method.

The fifties reveal a continuity and development of thinking with the work above, with the production of material related to social issues increasing. Janssens reflected the times, as he wrote on issues of justice, strikes, and the task of the state. He was widely published in the fifties, often in several journals whose interest was labor (see bibliography). It is significant that the first article dealing with the problems in marriage of periodic continence appeared very early, in 1952. While this piece was brief and was published in a rather lightweight journal, it marks a beginning. The decade would not end before the publication of his first substantial article on the subject in *Ephemerides*. Later we shall see the development in thinking, as well as the dedication to the tradition that Janssens possesses.

During this period his thinking on personalism would be

---

[50] See especially those which have appeared since the early 1960's in *Louvain Studies*.

greatly expanded. In addition to the 1957 publication of his book, mentioned above, several contemporaray articles reflect a personalist approach. His impact on the greater theological community begins to be felt, evidenced by the translation or duplicate publication of a significant portion of his work in French, Spanish, and English.

The shaking of the foundations that was going on in the greater church of the sixties found its aftershocks in Janssens' work of that period. At the beginning of the decade one might accurately have described him as the darling of married couples, as he produced no less than eight articles for *Huwelijk en huisgezin*, the Flemish equivalent of the American *Marriage Magazine*[51] written for Christian families. The darling of the Vatican he was not, however. With the publication of his more detailed and lengthy article in *Ephemerides* on the subject of conjugal morality and the other important work of this period on the topic, he caused a stir that would affect thinking in this area beyond the households of Belgium and would provoke a significant clerical reaction from Rochester to Rome. The effect of this backlash on Janssens himself was to be significant.

Other areas of his interest would find expression in the work of the council. It is not mere coincidence that his book on religious liberty came to publication at the precise time that the council fathers were wrestling with this issue. Within the year the book was produced in Spanish and within two there was an English translation.

The 1970's yielded more of Janssens' work in English translation. Through the efforts of Raymond Collins, its editor, *Louvain Studies* offered to the larger scholarly community for the first time a generous sample of the fruits of Jannsens' thinking. The seminal articles on personalist morality, ontic evil, and artificial insemination were published.

While the current decade is not over, there have been a significant number of publications produced at the secluded

---

[51] Now *Marriage and Family Living*.

house on Cardinal Mercier Lane. In retirement Janssens has continued to write on topics spanning in time such diversity as Thomas Aquinas and Lawrence Kohlberg. He has maintained his interest in medical and sexual topics and has provided reaction to the bishops synod on the family in 1980. He has published an update to his article on ontic evil. The new article answers in some detail the objections raised to his positions by Paul M. Quay.[52] The book in process goes slowly, however, as Janssens expects it to be his last. He has plans to be around for a good long time.

[52] "The Disvalue of Ontic Evil," *Theological Studies* 46 (1985) 262-286.

CHAPTER TWO

THE DEVELOPMENT OF AN APPROACH

From a review of Janssens' history, we can turn to a consideration of the foundations of his moral method.

The most consistent theme in Janssens' work and the basis for his moral methodology is the human person adequately considered. An incarnate spirit, the human person is a dynamic totality which tends toward its proper fulfillment. The human person is the essential element which grounds Janssens' method in all its aspects. The components are discernible in his major writings, even from the earliest period, and are echoed in others. Hints of the direction he will take are present in his patristic material, which appreciates the dignity of the human person as related to the incarnate word of God.[1]

The full explication of his methodology begins in his magister dissertation, *Personne et société*.[2] Time has seen erosion, underlining, or expansion of various aspects of the insights found here, but the basic method is already apparent.

---

[1] Since there is no much published material which in one way or another explains his personalist moral method, it is necessary to organize it in some fashion. We shall show the development of the method through the larger more significant works, especially major books.

[2] *Théories actuelles et essai doctrinal* (Dissertationes ad gradum magistri in Facultate Theologica vel in Facultate Iuris Canonici consequendum conscriptae, series II- Tomus 32), Gembloux: Duculot, 1939. Janssens himself does not value the work he did here. He feels it was done in too great a hurry (interview with Louis Janssens, 29 April 1986, Louvain, Belgium). Perhaps this criticism is valid with regard to the treatment of the various European ideologies. Careful reading of the more original portions of the work, however, reveals that even in 1939 the thrust of what would constitute his personalist moral method was already established. This is certainly the opinion of Jan Jans in his work, which refers in some depth to the method as described in *Personne et société*. See "De norm van de zedelijkheid de personalistische antropologie van Louis Janssens," Louvain, 1983 (Mimeographed).

Personne et société

Personne et société was published in 1939 as a Roman Catholic critique of several contemporary European ideologies. The first half of the book deals with the relationship of the human person to communism, fascism, and national socialism. In the final portion of the book Janssens responds with a picture of the human person in a Christian context. It is here that the foundation of his personalist moral method is introduced. In this early work Janssens treats his subject in three aspects: 1) the person as a totality, 2) personalist morality, and 3) the person as ordained toward God.

The Human Person as a Totality

Janssens describes the human person as totality, treated first as a substantial unity, an autonomous totality.[3] His point of departure is existential, beginning with the person as s/he exists and as s/he encounters the self. The person's immediate self perception is as an active totality, whose activities are special aspects or partial functions of that whole. "I walk, I eat, I see, I think: all these actions I ascribe spontaneously to the same 'I,' to the same totality."[4] These activities evidence a dynamic reciprocity: the actions I perform proceed from the abiding and recognizable person, but they serve as well to build or to create that person within the extending arena of time.

The person is a complex totality, a spirit in a body,[5] existing in a spatio-temporal universe. It is precisely and only through the body that the human being is able to unfold or actuate[6] his or

---

[3] *Personne et société*, p. 199. Translation mine. All subsequent translations are mine, unless otherwise indicated.

[4] Ibid.

[5] While this term is used frequently by Janssens, it is not original in his work.

[6] Janssens uses the French word, *épanouissement*, here, which connotes the blossoming of flowers, expansion, brightening (*Personne et société*, p. 200). One sees a connection, perhaps, to the notion of "lighting up" that Heidegger uses in *Being in Time*.

her human life. This bodily comportment toward the world is first of all physical in its exterior and material manifestations. The physical aspect is an impersonal moment, a particular portion, as it were, isolated in the spatio-temporal whole.[7] It does not in itself fully define the person. Rather, as Janssens comments, the nature of the person is embodied in a particularity, that is, in a limitedness bound to a certain point in time and space. This circumscription disallows ubiquitous or simultaneous attachment, identification, or comportment in other places and times. The activities of the physical body are concrete and categorical; it cannot be all, do all, nor be everywhere. To choose option "A" here and now precludes the simultaneous choice of option "B."

The body is not fully exterior, however. It has an interior component as well, which is the seat of both sense knowledge and sense appetite. This union with the internal human being is not a constant, but rather functions in response to stimuli given it. This is essential to the establishment of the individuality of the human person, however, because it enables the creative immanence of individuality and makes possible the particularity that is individuality.

Finally, the body is the source of the immanent operations of intellect and will. These operations function only through the situated bodily being. We see that Janssens considers the intellect and will from an existential perspective. He observes that the person is aware of the activities of intellect and will as nontemporal activities—my thoughts and desires are able to be present to other times and to other places or to draw them here. They are not bound by this place and this moment, even though they occur in a certain concrete here and now.

> Consideration of my intellectual and volitional activity forces me therefore to admit in myself a principle of life, which exerts its action within and by itself in an intrinsic independence with regard to my body. It is an active interiority, spontaneous, generative of unforeseen novelty, individualized and distinct from all the rest by its very originality ....[8]

[7] Ibid.
[8] Ibid., p. 203.

This "me" endures beyond the incremental becoming of the bodily existence of the human being. It is the interior center of the persistent person. This person is and perdures in time, and yet at the same time exists in and as a certain timeless, non-material entity. This paradoxical situation is foundational for certain considerations of subjective morality, which Janssens develops later in his exposition of ontic evil.

Janssens turns to a discussion of the activities of the human person as they proceed from the intellect and the will. The specifically human faculties of intellect and will are manifested in immanent activities which are both constitutive and creative of the human person.[9] "It is said rightly that the person reveals self in his/her activity and that this activity likewise reveals the person to him/herself."[10] This activity, a spiritual function, is situated in the "me" who is embodied and who moves toward perfection. There is both the infinite desire for knowledge and unlimited appetite for the good in tension with an ideal. The ideal stands before the activity, preceding its realization. Realization occurs through the concrete singular increments of choice the person makes in pursuit of the ideal. The ideal is actualized in so far as the person's choices are congruent to it. Janssens' treatment is evocative of the work of Blondel, especially in its use of polarities.[11] Janssens speaks of self knowledge, which seems to be independent. At the same time the self perceives its own dependence on something outside it. One determines oneself, yet one is incomplete in oneself. There is multiplicity in unity both in the intellect, a single capacity with many possible choices, and the will, an unlimited appetite—both with a set of possibilities for actualization limited by time and space. One cannot understand the being or the acting of the human person without simultaneously entertaining these polarities.

[9] See complete discussion, ibid., p. 212. Cf. Jan Jans, who follows closely Janssens' text here. See especially p. 16.

[10] *Personne et société*, p. 207.

[11] Blondel's work emphasizes the dialetic relationship that exists between the person and the environment. See Maurice Blondel, *The Letter on Apologetics and History of Dogma* (New York: Holt, Rinehart, and Winston, 1964).

Janssens turns to the consideration of human destiny. Since the human person is more than his/her body, it is necessary for the person to continue to create the self progressively in the arena of history. Says Janssens, "There is always a discrepancy between what a person is and what a person must be."[12] For the human person the "must be" is caught in the apparent paradox of his/her intrinsic limitation—with its inability to realize all but a few of the potentialities for becoming—and the pull to completion and perfection. We can detect here another instance of the seeds of Janssens' notion of ontic evil. The full blooming of the human person can be accomplished only in the infinite, says Janssens, and in humanity's terminus in eternity. Janssens demonstrates his unashamed preference for a Christian perspective.[13] Since the proper object of the intellect is all truth and the proper object of the will is all good, according to Thomas Aquinas,[14] the human person is fulfilled only in that which embodies all truth and all good, that is God. Janssens espouses a viewpoint of humanity that is essentially optimistic and religious. The person is essentially oriented toward the good and open to relationship with God, a viewpoint not always shared by those from other schools of personalism.[15]

Further, since Janssens is essentially an existentialist, he does not locate his method in other-worldly categories but inserts it in the real. For Janssens the concrete and temporal destiny of the human person *is* the human person; the potentiality and capacity for becoming oneself is achieved precisely in the value accomplished, that is, the actualized person. Says Janssens, "A person is

[12] *Personne et société*, p. 213.

[13] And to the philosophy of Blondel and the theology of Thomas, both of whom he mentions with some regularity. See, for example, ibid., p. 213.

[14] Janssens alludes to Thomas frequently. Often—here, for example—he does not cite specific passages, but presumes the reader's familiarity with the work of the angelic doctor. Where he does make specific reference to a text in Thomas, we shall so note.

[15] See discussion in Chapter One, especially pp. 16-17, on the various types of personalism. It is quite possible to embrace a so-called personalist thinking which denies a divine component in favor of the isolated self or the collective as the governing value.

a destiny: the person is form for self, value to be realized. For the person, to live, then, is to realize one's value as person."[16] This destiny is realized in a *"perpétuel devenir* (perpetual becoming)."[17] While the same person endures, that person is continually changing not only biologically but in the other facets of the personal comportment toward space and time.

The spatio-temporal mode places the human person into relationship with the rest of the universe. But more than that, the human person experiences the self in relationship to other human beings. These are very important in the development of the life of a human person. Following Thomas Aquinas, Janssens notes the political and social nature of the human being—one ordained to life in community.[18] The human being, unlike other animate creatures, is unable to satisfy completely his or her needs. Reason provides the tool to overcome this basic biological disadvantage. By the establishment of a linkage to other human beings for the mutual use of diverse talents, this tool can be maximized. In fact, this linkage is so important that "without life in community, a human being would not know how to fulfil his or her destiny."[19]

Following von Hildebrand,[20] Janssens distinguishes three categories of human social interaction. The first he calls social acts. This category includes interpersonal contracts. Between the two parties there is a common object which binds them in a necessary interaction, but this interaction has no emotional ties.

The second group likewise includes a common object outside the persons, but in this case the object (a work of art, for example) functions by evoking the same sentiment from each. The persons comprise a "we" as they participate in a subjective

[16] Ibid., p. 234.
[17] Ibid., p. 215.
[18] Ibid., p. 216. Cf. Thomas Aquinas, *Summa contra Gentiles*, I, III, c. 85.
[19] Ibid.,p. 217. Cf. Thomas Aquinas, *Summa contra Gentiles*, I, III, c. 117.
[20] Dietrich von Hildebrand, *Metaphysik der Gemeinschaft, Untersuchungen über Wesen und Wert der Gemeinschaft* (Augsburg, s.n., 1930) pp. 27-28; 39-42; 47-140.

togetherness in that which the object evokes, namely a sort of spiritual union.

The third category of human relationships is that of the "I" and the "Thou." Here the immediate goal of the relationship is not something external but rather the other person as such. "I value, I venerate, I love *someone*," says Janssens.[21] If the activity is mutual and reciprocal, there is a union between persons, based on their own intrinsic value. It is this union that founds human love. These ideas will serve later to ground Janssens' work on marriage.

How is such union possible? Or, for that matter, how can persons form any common bonds, even of the less intimate variety described above? Janssens presupposition is that a common world of values exists in which all persons participate. Each person comes to realize these values according to his or her own particularity, that is, according to the unique diversity and talent that each possesses. Values form a common pool which is the source of social possibility. If human beings are open to the world, they are likewise open[22] to the set of values that all other human beings find in their reality. It is this set of values that comprise the medium of union for people.[23] These ideas are foundational for his work in social justice.

These ideas likewise demonstrate an existential paradox. Union is possible and present in human community. It is experienced both as desire and as fulfillment. Yet the human person is always separate and distinct, a prisoner as it were within the shackles of the singularity of time and space. Transcendental humanity is intimately bound to existential humanity.

Although the themes that he plays here, as he himself points

---

[21] *Personne et societé*, p. 219.

[22] In fact, Janssens says that humanity is "essentially and objectively ordained to a world of values." Ibid., p. 220.

[23] The polarity demonstrated is expanded in many of Janssens' later works under the headings of objective and subjective culture. See for example *Droits personnels et autorité* (Louvain: Nauwelaerts, 1954), pp. 6, 40-42; "De rechen van de mens," *Tijdschrift voor politiek* 2 (1952) 525.

out, are not completely original with him, as his thinking matures he will develop them and make them his own. The various modes of relationship between and among persons are essential to the complete understanding of Janssens' moral methodology.

Having discussed the properties and activity of the human person, Janssens attempts a definition. He makes the distinction between the human person and the human being as individual. The person constitutes the human being in his or her totality. It is the ontological principle which penetrates and synthesizes the activity of the whole. It is the "*moi profond*"[24] from which flows thinking and willing, and which stretches under the collection of individual spatio-temporal acts to connect them to each other in a whole. It is this "consummate me" which constructs and achieves its own destiny in the activity of the whole.

The individual, on the other hand, is that aspect of the human being that is defined by its concrete position in time and space as distinct from other entities which also exist in time and space. The individual is enmeshed in the world, utilizing the things which surround it. The "*moi spirituel*" is hidden here, unique and distinct from others in its personal and interior activity. It is precisely because he or she is a person that one can be an individual. The individual is the same totality, which subsists as an individual because the being of the spiritual element is the being of the entirety. One is actualized as person in one's individuality. The person is an individuality "extended and intensified."[25] This definition has ramifications for the importance of time and space in moral thinking. The individually placed moral actions ultimately serve to define who the person is.

There exists, in addition to the self-creating entity moving in a spatio-temporal plane, a "me" that is not knowable to others nor completely even to self. It is known only to God, perceived as the

---

[24] Ibid., p. 224.

[25] Ibid., p. 227. The distinction between the individual and the person is made by Maritain, who distinguishes the individual as the material component and the person as the spiritual component of the human being. See p. 19 above.

author of being and of the particular being that is the unique human person.

The moral person

Janssens' personalist moral theology is grounded in the synthesis and unity of the specifically human functions: the intellect and the will. There is a harmony between the intellect's capacity and orientation toward truth and the will's assent in specific categorical action toward a congruence with good. When this is accomplished, the will acts, says Janssens, in a disinterested and objective fashion. The truth or the good exist apart from and independent of the person. Their claim on the person is by way of attraction. They exist outside the person both materially and motivationally. The task of the person in self achievement is to determine those activities which truly conform to the existence and development of the total personality as such. This is not a completely subjective activity, since the person is not fulfilled by self whim but seeks his or her destiny in the realization of truth and goodness in an objective sense. Janssens is quite clear on this point. He concludes:

> To sum up: to be a person is to posit self, to construct self, to perfect self and to accomplish one's destiny in a multiplicity of immanent activities; by virtue of the same immanence, the person or the totality as such is term, standard, and value for him/herself, and from that, the value of the person as such becomes the rule and standard of activity.... Practically, confronted with the complexity of values, the human being will have to ask him/herself: what is it that objectively is suitable to my personal totality in order to lead a life worthy of a person?[26]

The subjective choice of the person toward self achievement in this concrete situation, therefore, is not uninformed, but is elected in congruence to objective standards of what it means to be a human person. Janssens outlines those objective criteria which cannot be ignored. First, human life must be preserved in order

---

[26] *Personne et société*, p. 235.

to provide an adequate temporal span in which the person may concretize his or her destiny. This temporal existence, however, is always subordinate to the spiritual destiny of the human person, which can never be compromised even to save one's material life. Second, by reason of his or her materiality, the person implicates the material world in the journey toward his or her destiny. With the human person considered both in him/her self and in relationship as the starting point, one must assess the use of private property and the economic life in general, since they, too, are essential elements in the destiny of the human person. Third, since human beings are essentially ordered toward society, it is necessary to treat other persons in keeping with the same criteria that one would apply to oneself, that is, as a human person with an inviolable destiny. Fourth, in relationship to the community as such, one must study precisely what is the objective sense of the relationship between the person and the community. This objective sense does not remain static, since both the community and the persons within it are changing. Finally, an adequate idea of the objective value of the person and indeed of a personalist moral method is possible only with an understanding of the place of God. Janssens discusses this theme in some detail.

The Person in Relationship with God

Janssens' position here is not substantially different from that found in Blondel or in other contemporary personalist philosophers, namely that the human being is not the cause of his or her own existence, but rather is dependent on another for that existence. We experience ourselves as open to objective truth which exists outside ourselves and exerts a claim on our activity.[27] We experience ourselves as dependent. "I discover that I am neither the sole nor the primary principle of my activity," notes Janssens.[28] While the person seems capable of acting, the

[27] Ibid., p. 238.
[28] Ibid., p. 240.

direction of that action is experienced as imposed from outside the subject.[29]

Does this objective truth, then, impose upon persons an obligation? If I know what is true, independent of my subjective state, must I not conform my activities to that truth? Janssens would affirm the statement as presented. Key, however, is that I cannot know all truth. My temporal and spatial limitedness precludes such complete knowledge. While God and God's truth stand as our destiny, we must move toward that destiny by our own choices. "We determine our action, we choose our means."[30] Among the multiplicity of possibilities, each person has a limited set of concrete choices. These choices hinge on objective criteria, but ultimately the human person chooses concretely—although imperfectly—in the freedom which he or she enjoys.

In sum, the kernel of Janssens's method is already present in his earliest major work. *Personne et société* lays the foundation for a personalist moral method. Moral value is found in the human person adequately considered. To consider the person adequately one must examine the objective criteria as found in the meaning of the human person, in the relationships of that person, and especially in the relationship with the ultimate destiny of the person, that is, God. But from a personalist point of view, these objective criteria are always enfleshed, as it were, in the concrete reality—"the incarnate spirit"—that is the human person. Their ultimate meaning, their ultimate value for *this* person are discovered in the blooming of *this* human person. That discovery is possible only in the real activity which that person chooses.

The Middle Period

The later 1940's and 1950's witness Janssens' expansion of his

[29] Therefore, "I am not able to create the law which imposes itself on me; but I construct myself conforming or not conforming to the law." Ibid., p. 240

[30] Ibid., p. 243.

insights.[31] Representative articles and the major book of the period indicate that the method as it appears today was already well in place. Much of Janssens' work here deals with concrete moral issues.[32] Perhaps it is this application which catalyzes the systematization of his thinking and the detailed expansion of the earlier ideas. He concentrates on the underpinnings of his personalist method, namely the objective components.

Perhaps the most systematic treatment of the method of this period is to be found in his 1957 book, *Personalisme en democratisering* (Personalism and Democratization).[33] Janssens presents his "norm of morality" in dialogue with the philosophical foundations on which Christian personalism relies.[34] Jans notes that in earlier articles, "De rechten van de mens," for example, Janssens' had already explored to some extent the contents of the norm.[35] In *Personalisme en democratisering* he brings his thinking together in a single volume. Except for one short article, it is the only work he published in 1957.

In the first chapter of the book Janssens deals specifically with the norm of morality in his personalist methodology. He poses

---

[31] *Personne et société* can be considered a base line for Janssens' method. Later thinking in large measure flows from this initial wrestling with the ideas of a Christian personalism.

[32] See, for example, his articles on medicine, social work, and human rights that appear during these years. He appears to move away from the mostly pious articles which characterize, with few exceptions, the period between *Personne et société* and the late 1940's. More and more of his work appears in such socially oriented journals as *Kultuurleven* and *Politica-Berichten*. Even offerings in pastoral journals, seem to take on more concrete issues. See, for example, the 1956 article on situation ethics, "Moderne situatie-ethiek in het licht van de klassieke leer over het geweten," *Pastor Bonus* 33 (1956) 71-87.

[33] Brussels: Arbeiderspers, 1957. This book constitutes a synthesis of much of his thinking to date. Its first chapter is an expansion of "De norm van de zedelijkheid en de integriteit van de persoon," *Collectanea Mechliniensia* 41 (1956) 161-186. The second chapter, "De rechten van de persoon," was published much later in English in the *American College Bulletin* 38 (1959) 12-15; 113-121. Many of the ideas expanded here are found in other works of the same period.

[34] This statement is made by Jans, quoted from a Flemish journal in which Janssens' 1958 article "Christendom en geweten" appeared. See Jans, p. 40.

[35] Jans, ibid.

the question: how can we verify the statement, the moral good is that which is in keeping with the objective sense of our "being-as-person" (*persoon-zijn*) in the natural and supernatural order?[36] He begins with familiar ideas from his earlier work, namely the adequate consideration of the human person. The human person, we recall, is an open interiority, experiencing self in the concrete moments of human activity. Human activity is both immanent and transcendent. Its end is not limited to its material existence. Rather it has a supernatural terminus, the endpoint of its *capacitas infiniti*.[37] By baptism the Christian enters into a supernatural relationship, a community, with the persons of the Trinity. This relationship is intimate, the presence of the Holy Spirit within the person. [38]

Janssens seeks to establish a personalistic norm of morality, an objective sense. Objectivity is essential to the method, which has been criticized so often as a surrender to the purely subjective, that is a form of situation ethics. To understand Janssens' method is to see clearly that it is not a collapse into subjectivity, but rather rests on the objective criteria that are demonstrated here. These objective criteria are the contents of the moral norm, namely the person considered in relationship and the person considered in self.

The Person in Relationship

Relationship to God

First, the person is related dependently and essentially to God. "Our absolute dependence upon God is written in all the manifestations of our existence," notes Janssens.[39] It is recognized, or more precisely, it is discovered by persons in their relationship to the things of the material world, which possesses what he calls a trace or trail (*spoor*)[40] of God within, and more directly, as

---

[36] *Personalisme en democratisering*, p. 5.
[37] Ibid., p. 22.
[38] Ibid., p. 24.
[39] *Droits personnels et autorité*, p. 10.
[40] See *Personalisme en democratisering*, p. 29.

related to other human beings themselves.[41] The former are the gifts of God to humanity, gifts that are essential to true human perfection. It is in relationship to these gifts that the human being begins to discover the objective sense of his or her relationship to God, that is, God's will.

In other human beings as in oneself, God's image is discovered.[42] For Janssens, this divine image is, for Janssens, the most fundamental expression of the objective sense of the human person. It is not a static expression; rather it confronts the person as a dynamic vocation, a never completed task.[43] As the human person actualizes the possibilities of thought and free will in actions s/he becomes more and more the image and likeness of God. What this means concretely—the objective contents of this image and likeness—is discovered by the person in his or her existence as interiority and openness.

This activity has both a formal and a material content. The formal content is expressed in the essential direction of the human person toward perfection in the image of God. All that we do must be inspired by our religious disposition and by our love of God, notes Janssens.[44] Elsewhere he expresses the idea more passionately, stating that our actions should be drenched (*doordrenkt*) in the love of God.[45] The material content is expressed in the concrete activities of the person. The real moral perfection of the person, that is, the actualization of the will of God for the person, coincides with making progress in becoming more and more the image of God. Therefore relationship with God includes

[41] In his book Janssens treats his ideas more formally than do other works of the same period. He draws frequently on Thomas Aquinas, in this instance citing his teaching on the participation of God in creation (see *Summa Theologica*, I, q. 44, art. 4). The idea grounds the expansion of Janssens' thought (see *Personalisme en democratisering*, pp. 28-29).

[42] Ibid., p. 29.

[43] Things of this world are both gift and mission, notes Janssens. See "De rechten van de mens," p. 527. This passage is translated and expanded in *Droits personnels et autorité*, p. 9.

[44] *Personalisme en democratisering*, p. 32.

[45] "Recht en moraal," *Sint-Lucasblad* 28 (1956) 529.

an obligation to seek out the objective sense of being-as-person, that is as an openness and interiority. Through the capacity to think and through divine revelation, persons are able to expose and respond to the objective sense of what this means.[46]

The relationship to the things of this world

As noted above, the human person as an incarnate spirit must rely on the things of the world to realize his or her own possibilities for fulfillment and perfection. S/he is "essentially thrown"[47] into the world. Janssens' ideas seem to follow closely Heidegger's development in *Being and Time*.[48] The things of the world are discovered as means to the end of human perfection. This is the objective sense of things. Says Janssens:

> ... our relations to the world manifest a fundamental and objective sense, which we do not create, but which is given to us and which we discover in our very existence in as much as it is open to the world: things are our means.[49]

The human person develops self from the perspective of his/her essential openness and through active contact with the things of this world.[50] This contact is dynamic and dialectic. There is a dialogue between what I create of myself for myself from my unique capacity and diverse possibilities (subjective culture) by drawing from the world's heritage of wisdom and technology, and that which I in turn contribute to the ongoing deposit of culture in the world (objective culture).[51] The person cannot

---

[46] In this book Janssens assumes and dialogues with the Christian perspective. He sees the entire moral life as having a religious meaning. See *Personalisme en democratisering*, p. 30.

[47] "De rechten van de mens," p. 524.

[48] See pp. 82-83. Heidegger sees the destiny of *Dasein* as Being-in-the-world bound to "those entities which it encounters within its own world." Being-in-the-world is "an essential structure of *Dasein*."

[49] "Les bases du personnalisme," *Service sociale dans le monde* 14 (1954) 51.

[50] *Personalisme en democratisering*, p. 32.

[51] Here Janssens takes up a theme evident in much of his work of this period. See *Personalisme en democratisering*, pp. 32-34. Cf. "De rechten van de mens,"

actualize his or her own possibilites without relying on the things of the world. Janssens points out that in the essential reciprocity between the objective and subjective culture lies the fundamental sense of our relationship to the things of the world. [52]

It is essential to emphasize that this activity represents real development. As the person's activity contributes in an immediate fashion to the objective culture, he or she contributes in a distant fashion to his or her own subjective culture. What is contributed is a real advancement, something that was not a part of the existential horizon before.

Our relationship of person to person

Our relationship to other people differs from our relationship to things. There exists between persons, says Janssens, "a deeper reciprocity, a dialogue in the full sense of the word." [53] They can communicate thoughts, feelings, and values. In dialogue with others the human person learns that the other is a subject like oneself and therefore must be treated as a self, a neighbor. [54] This realization brings the person to the understanding that the other cannot be treated as an object, as merely another thing at hand, [55] but must be approached as an "originality" (*oorspronkelijkheid*), an irreplaceable interiority (*onvervangbare innerlijkheid*). [56]

The attitude unfolds in a loving treatment of the other, a

p. 525; and *Droits personnels et autorité*, pp. 5-9. These ideas are present already in *Personne et société*. See pp. 290-313.

[52] *Personalisme en democratisering*, p. 33.

[53] Ibid., p. 34.

[54] This word has the connotation of the English "bosom buddy" or the Latin "alter ego." It is *evennaste* in Dutch, a "delicious Flemish word," as Janssens explains in some detail in his 1951 radio talk, "Liefde en sociaal leven" (Antwerp: t'Groit, 1951), p. 8. The ideas expressed in this talk follow quite closely the themes of *Personalisme en democratisering*.

[55] Again and again the likeness to the thinking of Martin Heidegger is echoed in Janssens' work. Cf. *Being and Time*, pp. 153-154.

[56] See *Personalisme en democratisering*, p. 35. Cf. "Liefde en sociaal leven," pp. 8-9. Here Janssens roots this approach in the scriptural admonition to love one's neighbor as oneself. This notion is at the base of Janssens' so-called "love ethics," which he develops more fully later on.

disposition that is both aloof and interested. This aloofness does not mean a lack of care;[57] rather it suggests that human love at its best is not possessive but freeing and interested in the proper goals of the other rather than the goals of the self. In this way the other person is aided in the fulfillment of him or her self.[58] Love stands radically opposed to a thrust or desire or impulse for possession, notes Janssens.[59] Real love is actualized in a reciprocity, the result of which is the fulfillment of both parties in the relationship. The norm of morality for relationship between persons, then, is the objective sense of those persons, namely their existence as subjects, to be treated as other selves.

Always practical, Janssens underlines the importance of the real. Concrete acts (objective realities) are necessary in order to make love real. The effective meaning of love is lost if not incarnated in exterior deeds, in real development.[60] The mere intention of love (subjective element) remains hidden in the interiority of the person if not expressed in real deeds.

The relationship to society

Again Janssens emphasizes a dialectic relationship, in this case between the person and society. There is a real reciprocity between the person and the community in which he or she exists. On the one hand, society provides certain things that precede and are essential to the human person. From the very beginnings of life the human person is social. We do not create our own situation. It is given in the same way our bodiliness is given. Within this given we are able to discover ourselves as a result of our relationships.[61] Society provides both the milieu and the content that allows the development of the components of humanity. Without society there is no humanity. As a child embarks

[57] Indeed, Janssens' ideas point to a sense of care congruent to the *fürsorge* of Heidegger. See *Being and Time*, especially pp. 157, 237, and 238.

[58] *Personalisme en democratisering*, pp. 36-37.

[59] "Liefde en sociaal leven," p. 8.

[60] *Personalisme en democratisering*, pp. 37-38.

[61] Ibid., p. 45.

into life, s/he is an open intentionality. The child becomes in response to the environment, finding its own self consciousness, and developing into a reflexive consciousness.

On the other hand, the human person has a choice of disposition toward this environment. The basic freedom of the human person comes precisely in the free acceptance of his or her situation.[62] Further, the person may choose from a variety of possibilities in social life and can ask questions about the objective sense of this involvement, this relationship between person and society.

The goal and mission of personal involvement in the tasks of society is the achievement of the common good. The genuine community, says Janssens, is the "we" of a conscious and free collaboration on the communal task, aimed at the realization of the common good.[63] Since the individual person is limited both by lack of time and by an incomplete set of capacities, and since the pool of individuals within the community offers a much broader pool of diverse talents and possibilities, such collaboration is essential to the optimal realization of the values within the objective culture. Says Janssens, "Diversity unites us and constitutes in society the source of the richness of life."[64]

While this realization is the immediate goal of the communal task, the secondary result is the achievement of subjective culture, that is the individual perfection of each member of the society. It is this task that is the most important in a personalistic system.[65] Society must always realize objective cultural values "in view of the subjective culture of all and of each."[66] This personal realization is essentially dependent on the preceding goal of social advancement. Human sociability "is not something accessory."[67]

---

[62] In later articles Janssens will develop this idea further, using a more Rahnerian frame of reference as he speaks of "fundamental choice." See, for example, "Personalist Morals," *Louvain Studies* 3 (1970-71) 9.

[63] *Personalisme en democratisering*, p. 48.

[64] *Droits personnels et autorité*, p. 16.

[65] For Janssens the baseline for drawing conclusions in his method is always the human person. It is the standard against which all is measured.

[66] "Philosophie sociale," *Service social dans le monde* 14 (1955) 50.

[67] *Droits personnels et autorité*, p. 18.

The interaction between objective and subjective culture is a real activity, an historical reality. As such it creates genuine progress over the span of history, progress for the individual in the existential realization of perfection and progress for the community in the real addition of objective values to the cultural pool. Says Janssens, "In this way the objective culture of yesterday becomes the source of the subjective culture of today, and the latter is the vital soil on which an enriched objective culture shall prosper tomorrow."[68] This process is never complete, but rather continues through time in the arena of history.

In addition the process is a social reality. It is nourished by the real interest and involvement of individual persons who, as subjects, take a stance in their intentionality and openness toward the world, toward other people as subjects, and toward God.[69] Underlying societal relationships there is a social love,[70] analogous to the love between subjects that is essential to interpersonal relationships. This love informs the elements that undergird and move societies: 1) to regulate relationships between people in a healthy community,[71] 2) to accomplish the working together of all people for the achievement of objective culture, 3) to insure that the objective culture works toward the realization of subjective culture.[72] The object of social justice is precisely the set of

[68] "Recht en moraal," p. 522.

[69] See *Personalisme en democratisering*, p. 53.

[70] This theme of love, so strongly underlined in his 1951 radio talk, becomes more and more developed as the years progress. It reaches center stage in "Norms and Priorities in a Love Ethics," *Louvain Studies* 6 (1976-77) 207-238. Further, it will be the basis for the first chapter in a book on his methodology, currently in progress.

[71] In *Personalisme en democratisering* Janssens uses the term *gemeenschap*, which means "connection, communication, or community" (p. 62). In a parallel list in "Recht en moraal," p. 523, he uses instead *samenleving*. The latter can be translated literally as "together-living," a word much more graphic in its expression of the nature of community. It is especially apt in parallel with his use of *samenwerking* (together-working) in the second element.

[72] Elsewhere Janssens notes that there must be an ordering of the various values of the objective culture so that they may inform the subjective culture. See "De rechten van de mens," p. 526. It is impossible to achieve all the values possible in objective culture. Again, the bottom line for Janssens is always the

demands of social love. Social justice is experienced in the concrete expression of social love. "To fulfill and enrich our moral interiority we must be faithful to the objective sense of social intentionality," states Janssens.[73]

The Person

In this following section of *Personalisme en democratiserung* Janssens takes up in some detail the ideas that he set forth in his 1939 work, namely the consideration of the person in him/herself.

The person as spiritual interiority (innerlijkheid)

The first experience of the human being is of the self in action. I, for example, am able to read a book and at the same time remain conscious of both the *contents* of my reading and the *fact* that I am reading. I can hold both these ideas beyond their actual point in time. For Janssens these activities are disinterested actions, merely observations of the facts as they are present. The subject is a disinterested witness in this initial experience to what is there, over against subjective self interest. This deposit of fact, as it were, forms the basis for evaluation of moral activity of the subject, that is, the conscience. It is in this human spiritual interiority that we locate the ability to perceive the objective sense of our relations and of our self.[74]

Secondly, as a thinking and willing interiority the person is a free subject. This freedom is manifested in both the choice of ends toward which one might move and the means used to attain a

human person before all else. The perfection of the human person is the standard that orders the values for objective culture.

[73] *Personalisme en democratisering*, p. 63. Further development of the connection between justice and morality can be found in "Recht en moraal," pp. 524-530, especially.

[74] In the previous section Janssens has approached his theme from observation of the environment *outside* the person. Here he pursues the epistemology of this data. He concludes that the human person is capable of apprehending the objective sense of him/herself as well as that of the environment. His presupposition does not preclude, however, either the conscious or the unconscious neglect of this data. See *Personalisme en democratisering*, p. 64.

particular end. Although every person has a tendency toward choices which can become dissolved into selfishness, there still exists in the disinterested field of thinking a set of values which offer an objective standard over against this selfishness. We can aim at a variety of objects, judging which fit with the objective sense of who we are. We can use a variety of means, again in keeping with objective standards.

The concrete choices we make represent a real cultural progress. As we choose from the set of offerings available to us in the pool that is the objective culture, we create something new in our subjective culture which, in turn, contributes to the pool of objective culture. Our choices, however, are always limited. We are not creative in the sense that God is, but what we achieve has a creative element by means of the concrete choices we make among possibilities.

For Janssens, these choices are in conformity with the moral ideal[75] and thus with God's will, when they are made in a disinterested fashion. Over the "moments of time" (*de momenten van de tijd*)[76] we are able to create our own destiny. We can escape from our selfishness and selfish inclinations, says Janssens. We grow toward "a permanent liberation that is the conquest of our freedom."[77]

Within the person one can describe elements of the moral action which are important to his method. They are consistent with the thinking of Aquinas, as is patent to any student of scholasticism. There are three essential elements in the consideration of the human act: the aim (*streving*) or intention, the end of the agent (*doel*),[78] and the real good actualized by the action

[75] Janssens does not see this moral ideal as absolutely unchanging, however. As the culture progresses, more and more new elements enter the decision-making arena of human persons. These elements take the form of new values, which place a new set of objective standards before the person. The contents of morality, then, as well as the cultural contents, are progressive. See "Recht en moraal," p. 527.

[76] *Personalisme en democratisering*, p. 69.

[77] *Personalisme en democratisering*, p. 69.

[78] The Dutch word here can mean, among other things, the purpose, aim, or object. The connotation tends to link the word with the agent, however, rather than with something purely external (as the term "*goed*" does). Janssens uses it as

(*goed*).[79] Love (aim) motivates a husband to provide a living for his wife and children (end), while at the same time a product (good/concrete object) is produced which contributes in a real sense to the objective culture. Note the essential connection between the intention of the agent and the end here. This link, characteristic of Janssens and often missed in an analysis of his work, is the linchpin of his personalistic method. It places the moral weight of the action on the congruence between these two elements.[80]

Outside the person there exists the objective value that is also an essential consideration. If an action begins with the aim or intention, there must be certain qualities in a given object that lure the person. First, there may be qualities within the object which are congruent with the yearning within (e.g. thirst seeks for water). Secondly, however, there must be qualities which, says Janssens, are "suitable" to the totality of the person.[81] (Satisfaction of thirst after surgery, for example, may be harmful to the total bodily well being.) Ultimately, the sensate yearning must be subordinate to intentional affectivity, which must be aimed at the objective truth that embodies the totality of the human person.

For the individual person, this objective reality of self is experienced first of all as a horizon of possibility. The real experiences that push toward this horizon themselves serve to modify the totality in a concrete and unique fashion. The choices made in this direction, however, must serve the whole and not work only for the satisfaction of certain parts. It is the disinterested knowing conscience that directs these choices. Conscience can view a deed as conformity to the objective sense of the person or deviation from it. The latter produces a sadness in the person. Janssens speaks of the remorse of conscience as an "alarm-bell"

one would the English "end" to refer to the purpose or term desired by the agent. A further discussion of this point will be found in chapter three, below.

[79] Ibid., p. 69. Janssens' use of this term is equivalent to the English "actualized value."

[80] The complete explication of the ideas here are treated later in his Louvain Studies article, "Ontic Evil and Moral Evil," *Louvain Studies* 4 (1972-73) 115-156.

[81] *Personalisme en democratisering*, p. 70.

(*noodklok*),[82] which signals the need to recover the damaged entity.

Within the freedom of the person there can be a gradual movement toward virtue through repeated actions in conformity to the objective sense of the person. Each action placed in congruence with the objective sense of the whole entity, rather than in satisfaction in response to the separate strivings of the various parts of the individual, is an action in service of virtue. Virtue ultimately is the liberating force which frees the person from slavery to affectivity alone. Virtue disposes freedom in effective integration toward objective moral values.

Finally, the person is responsible—the third characteristic of personal interiority. Flowing from human freedom, responsibility calls the person to justify his/her free deeds over against the standard of conscience. This activity causes the person to define his/her own moral contents. Independent, I make my choices freely in conformity with the vision I see. Irreplacable, only I may use my own unique freedom in deciding who I shall become or not become. Inviolable, I am a subject not an object. In my interiority I must be allowed to function to achieve my own becoming. These principles ground Janssens' thinking on religious freedom, which is fully developed in later works.[83]

The person as bodily being (*lichamelijkheid*)

Janssens explores the relationship of the bodily reality of the human person to an objective norm of morality in order to further establish objective standards for moral action. He notes three aspects. First, life is a fact. This fact is the first and most essential condition for our moral destination. We achieve our destiny precisely in and through our bodily existence. Life is a valuable gift, one that may not be violated. On the other hand,

[82] Ibid., p. 77.

[83] The obvious example is *Liberté de conscience et liberté religieuse* (Paris-Bruges: Desclée de Brouwer, 1964), although the ideas are found in a number of other places in Janssens' corpus.

each life is subservient to our moral destination; therefore we are not free to act against its objective sense, that is, its destiny.

Secondly, life endures over a particular period of time. Our lifetime (*levenduur*)[84] is the given frame in which our destiny is to be achieved in the total series of concrete acts. We are bound then, in an objective sense, to do what we can to preserve this period, not to shorten it. On the other hand, we are not bound to do everything for ourselves (extraordinary means) in order to preserve this period of time unreasonably, since our limitedness precludes the actualizing of a complete set of possibilites for preservation. If I choose "A," I have rejected "B." If "A" represents the total set of actions necessary to preserve life indefinitely and "B" represents the total set of other actions I may perform, commitment to "A" precludes my doing anything else with my life.

Third, the body has various parts and capabilites which participate in every increment of being-as-person. We are bound to the specific conditions of the body in every activity. It is the exterior manifestation of the self to other persons, in service to the community in the creation of culture, in the specifically sexual activity betwen couples, and in the relationship we sustain with God. Janssens had spoken of this bodiliness in his earlier work.[85] The full bloom of the ideas is to be found here. First, to reach out to another in love, it is necessary to perform acts of love: signs, deeds, service. These acts are none other than bodily acts, dependent on the fleshy form through which each particular human being stands out to another. "Our body is the necessary means of our relationship with another, the bridge by which our love reaches others."[86]

Secondly, social advancement is the fruit of societal work, which flows only through the activities of the body. All work is the child of spirit and body, notes Janssens.[87] The body is—in a

---

[84] *Personalisme en democratisering*, p. 86.
[85] Cf. *Personne et société*, pp. 235-237.
[86] *Personalisme en democratisering*, p. 88.
[87] Ibid., p. 88.

sense—the tool by which we serve society, but it is a unique tool that is an imperishable share in the social cultural task.

Third, in the expression of sexuality, the body participates in a central way. The sexual organs influence the whole person. They possess a finality which belongs to the being of the whole person.[88] The concrete application of what is here a comparatively minor theme is seen in later articles on human sexuality, some of which provoked an uproar in the Catholic community.

Finally, Janssens points out the connection between human bodiliness and relationship to God. It is through the body that humanity relates to God, in worship, in sacrament, as temples of the holy spirit, and in suffering.

In order to illustrate the principles he has established, Janssens applies them here in a rather concrete fashion to the area of medical transplantation. It is one thing to speak in a general way about the basic components of the human person as openness and interiority, it is quite another—and perhaps a threatening thing—to begin to apply these ideas to concrete moral situations. In Roman Catholic moral theology this new way is to be considered both wonderful and woeful. On the one hand, the method offers a framework for tackling the new problems raised in the rapidly evolving fields of medicine and, especially, in human sexuality. On the other hand, a personalist moral method appears to provide the potential for new understandings of old problems, perhaps even new conclusions. As we deal with some of the specific areas to which Janssens' method has been applied this will become clear.

In sum, an examination of what we have termed the middle period of Janssens' work provides a deeper insight into his moral method. A gradual synthesis emerges and the personalistic themes which he first presented in his early *Personne et société* begin to blossom. He develops more completely the objective sense of the human being adequately considered as being-in-the-world, related as s/he is to others, to society, and to God. The human person as

[88]   Ibid., p. 89.

s/he is constituted and as s/he exists in relationship is the true "norm of morality." This norm, however, is not static but evolving, dependent on real historical and spatial possibilities. Janssens is developing a Christian religious personalism, so he situates this norm ultimately in the will of God, present in the world and in the person. Janssens expands the notion of objective and subjective culture, making it clear and applying it to problems of relationships within society. Finally, the importance of the limited bodiliness of the human being is presented more completely, laying foundations upon which will be built the structure of the concept of ontic evil.

Janssens in épanouissement

In the period following the publication of *Personalisme en democratisering*, Janssens' work comes to full bloom.[89] His moral methodology does not change to any great degree during these years. It is more nuanced in certain areas, especially as Janssens responds to contemporary reactions to his personalist method. What is more evident is the application to specific moral issues and the clarity with which he posits the normative aspects of his method. During the late fifties and early sixties he frequently addresses specific problems of practical significance. He publishes numerous articles in the popular journal *Huwelijk en huisgezin* (Marriage and Family) on the various aspects of Christian marriage, for example, and provokes a strong reaction among physicians—generally negative—when he writes a series of articles on morality in medicine in a local newspaper during a strike of Flemish doctors early in 1964.[90] Perhaps the greatest contribution to practical questions during this time, however, and certainly that which elicited the strongest response in both the

---

[89] It is appropriate to apply to Janssens the term he uses to refer to the accomplishment of the human person. See *Personne et société*, p. 200, for example.

[90] See below, chapter five.

scholarly community and the population at large, is the development and change in his thinking on the regulation of human conception.

During this period Janssens' interest in the temporal and spatial aspects of morality is made concrete in what may be his best known article, "Ontic Evil and Moral Evil."[91] Although a complete treatment of his thinking on the matter will be left for a later chapter, we will note the elements of historical and spatial considerations that are apparent in the methodological work of this period.

The cultural questioning of structures and values that characterized the early 1960's and that were brought into ecclesial focus at the Second Vatican Council, provided a creative field for Catholic thinking, conserving the rich heritage of a past and bringing it to bear in language and application for the modern world. For Louis Janssens the council documents and some contemporary papal statements[92] provided a certain validation for his own thinking as well as a forum for introducing his personalist method to a wider audience.[93] In his articles "Considerations on *Humanae Vitae*"[94] and "Artificial Insemination: Ethical Considerations,"[95] especially, Janssens painstakingly references his own thinking to the conciliar constitution *Gaudium et Spes*. Even a cursory reading of that document alongside Janssens' work affirms the close connections between the two. The familiar base line of the human person adequately considered does not go unnoticed. It is no accident that the theological ideas

[91] *Louvain Studies* 4 (1972-73): 115-156. An update on his thinking was published fifteen years later: "Ontic Good and Evil - Premoral Values and Disvalues," *Louvain Studies* 12 (1987) 62-82.

[92] The notable exception, of course, is the encyclical *Humanae Vitae*, which does not reflect a particularly personalistic perspective. As one might expect, Janssens reacts at some length to this document, as we shall see.

[93] The encyclical of Pope John XXIII *Mater et Magistra*, for example, provided such an opportunity. See Janssens' articles "*Mater et magistra*: voor een beter inzicht in de sociale encycliek van Paus Johannes XXIII," 15 May 1961 (Pamphlet); and "*Mater et Magistra*" *Vita-documentatie* 3 (1962) 3-12.

[94] *Louvain Studies* 2 (1968-69) 231-253.

[95] *Louvain Studies* 8 (1980-81) 3-29.

seeded and nurtured among the bishops and theologians who gathered to exchange ideas at 95 Cardinal Mercier Lane bear resemblance to the fruit produced in the council documents.

A major contribution from this time is *Liberté de conscience et liberté religieuse*,[96] made available to the council fathers for their discussions in preparation for *Dignitatis Humanae*. While history appears to credit this document principally to John Courtney Murray of the United States, there are those who believe that much of the foundation for this text is to be found in the thinking of Louis Janssens.[97]

These years are marked by a wider reading of his work, due largely to the influence of Dutch speaking theologians at the council and to the translation of much of his work into other languages.[98] The introduction of his thinking on regulation of birth into the United States in 1964 in no small way increased his notoriety.[99]

There is, however, no single book from this period that collates the basic elements of his thinking in quite the way we have seen in earlier periods. Among his more significant articles the most important may be "Personalist Morals," published in translation in 1970.[100] This article is rather brief, but it contains the elements of the method and serves as an accurate reflection of his thinking

[96] Paris-Bruges: Desclée de Brouwer, 1964.

[97] Conversation with people at the University of Leuven, Belgium, bears this out. Regretfully, however, the proof of this connection appears to have been buried with the destruction by his family of the papers of Victor Heylen after his death. Interview with Jan Jans, 28 April 1986, Louvain, Belgium.

[98] The considerable exposure of Janssens' work to an English speaking audience is largely the result of his frequent publication in *Louvain Studies* from the late 1960's up until the present.

[99] " ... the roar of canon' was again heard," notes Francis Swift, "An Analysis of the American Theological Reaction to Janssens' Stand on The Pill," *Louvain Studies* 1 (1966) 19. This double entendre referred to the publication of *Canon* Janssens' "Morale conjugale et progestogènes," *Ephemerides Theologicae Lovanienses* 39 (1963) 787-826.

[100] *Louvain Studies* 3 (1970-71) 5-16. This translation from the French by John L. Sullivan is the only published form of the article. It does not reflect in sequence (although certainly in content it does) the section in *Personne et société* of the same name. It is essentially a summary of the contents of Janssens' course, although the approach is somewhat different. Interview with Jan Jans, ibid.

in a more contemporary period, especially against the background of the historical development within the church.[101]

As Jans points out,[102] the article organizes the method into five themes,[103] none of which is entirely new. The first theme treats the intentionality of the human person as an open and relational reality.[104] There is an uncharacteristic reference in the text to Martin Heidegger, where Janssens notes the congruence of Heidegger's thinking to his own personalist method.[105] Janssens makes the distinction in this article between what he calls here primary and secondary relationships among persons.[106] The themes of the distinction between I-Thou type (friendship, conjugal and family relationships) and those objectively governed (exchange of goods and services) are not new, however. They have already been explored in earlier works. Reprise of the distinction of the reality outside ourselves in the form of objective culture and subjective culture is evident as well.[107]

The second theme is that of human intentionality as flowing from the subject, a conscious interiority.[108] A certain freshness of thinking is apparent, as Janssens refashions the basic ideas of his method—fairly constant over a span of thirty years—in the mode of more modern thinkers. Here he refers to the smiling game

---

[101] Janssens himself refers to this article, along with *Personalisme en democratisering* as representative of his method. See "Artificial Insemination: Ethical Considerations," p. 3, note 1.

[102] "De norm de zedelijkheid de personalistische antropologie van Louis Janssens," p. 89.

[103] These five themes are taken up again and expanded into eight in the later article on artificial insemination. It is clear from the parallels that there is little advancement in the basic method in the decade that separates the two articles. The changes are largely due to the emphasis demanded by the topic of the particular article.

[104] Cf. "Artificial Insemination: Ethical Considerations," pp. 6-7. Here the ideas are treated as themes 4 and 5.

[105] "Personalist Morals," p. 5.

[106] Cf. "Norms and Priorities in a Love Ethics," *Louvain Studies* 6 (1976-77) 222.

[107] Ibid., pp. 222-224.

[108] Cf. "Artificial Insemination: Ethical Considerations," p. 5. In this article this is the first theme.

between mother and child, a likely allusion to the work of Erik Erikson.[109] The subject is both conscious and free. The first, as we have seen, opens the human person to all reality, so that "in our knowing we transcend ourselves ...."[110] Yet the person is limited to the scope of his or her real relationships, although not completely defined by them. The question of human destination in God is treated under this section, different from what had been the case in *Personalisme en democratisering*, where the divine destination of the human person is treated as a separate section.[111]

In his or her self awareness the human subject is free as well. Our being "belongs to itself, it disposes of itself, it is its own task of self-fulfillment."[112] This freedom is, first of all, ontological; that is, it is represented in the fundamental choice a person makes or in the enduring state of fundamental intention. In his discussion of this fundamental orientation to freedom, Janssens demonstrates the concrete application of his personalist thinking to the area of religious freedom—a theme on which he concentrates during this period. The ontological freedom of the person is the source of his or her categorical freedom, the ability to actualize this or that possibility in a succession of particular actions. Janssens calls this "the foundation of historicity."[113] These ideas are in harmony with the thinking of Karl Rahner.[114]

The third theme taken up in "Personalist Morals" is that of the

---

[109] "Personalist Morals," p. 7. Cf. Erik H. Erikson, "The Development of Ritualization," in *The Religious Situation* (Boston: Beacon Press, 1968) p. 713; cited by George S. Worgul, *From Magic to Metaphor: A Validation of the Christian Sacraments* (New York: Paulist, 1980) p. 54.

[110] "Personalist Morals," p. 8.

[111] See *Personalisme en democratisering*, pp. 28-32. Cf. "Artificial Insemination: Ethical Considerations," p. 9 (Theme 6).

[112] "Personalist Morals," p. 9.

[113] Ibid., p. 11.

[114] See, for example, Rahner's synthetic work, *Foundations of Christian Faith* (New York: Seabury, 1968) p. 96. He states: " ... but in our passage through the multiplicity of the temporal we are performing this event of freedom, we are forming the eternity which we ourselves are and are becoming."

bodiliness of the human person.[115] Human beings are dependent on the material world and its own laws for their needs (air, food, etc.). The most basic dependence is that of the physical body itself, since it exists as a part of the material world.[116] Janssens' summarizes points that have been expanded in greater detail in earlier works, such as the dependence of all relationships on the bodily disposition toward the world. He concludes the section on this third theme by summarizing what he calls the "first universally valid moral principle:"

> good actions are those which objectively, i.e., in truth, in the light of reason and faith, correspond to the human person adequately considered—i.e. as an incarnate spirit, as a subject who, in its bodily condition, is conscious interiority and intentional openness to the world, to others, to God. Special morals explicitates the various aspects of this fundamental norm which states, generally, the entire content of morals.[117]

The fourth theme is the originality of the person.[118] The juxtaposition of the elements of basic human equality and individual human originality is not unfamiliar at this point. Both these poles must be maintained if one is to avoid dissolution into situation ethics on the one hand and an impersonal appeal to static standards on the other. Personalism, notes Janssens, maintains both the universal validity of moral norms that express the common aspects of both human and Christian meaning and the necessity to affirm the unique situation of each person in the concrete acts of his/her personal existence. This idea is key to Janssens' method. From the preservation of this polar tension flows Janssens second fundamental norm: "each and every person must fulfill himself [herself] according to his [her] personal originality."[119] Janssens hastens to add that the fulfillment of

[115] Cf. "Artificial Insemination: Ethical Considerations," pp. 5-6 (Theme 2).

[116] Ibid., pp. 6-7 (Theme 3).

[117] "Personalist Morals," p. 12.

[118] "Artificial Insemination: Ethical Considerations," pp. 12-13 (Theme 8).

[119] "Personalist Morals," p. 14. In "Artificial Insemination: Ethical Considerations" Janssens expands the two principles set forth here to what he calls the "personalist criterion." The ideas are the same basically, but his middle term in the

personal originality is accomplished within the context and on the basis of shared fundamental equality—a statement of confidence in the importance (not necessarily the applicability) of universal norms. These universal norms are themselves limited, as Janssens cautions, since the call of originality may draw persons beyond their horizon, demanding action "which the universal norms no longer express."[120] Personalism affirms the valid insight in situation ethics, which is neglected in classical morals, notes Janssens.[121] "This is one reason personalism considers as its norm the human person' rather than human nature.'"[122]

The final theme treated is human historicity.[123] It is interesting to see this idea elevated to one of the five central themes of Janssens' method. Since human culture is an historical reality and progress is always possible, it is possible to speak of a progress in morals. Morality seeks to respond to the actualization of new economic, scientific, and technical advancements, "to define the way in which these new acquisitions are to be integrated into individual and social existence, in order to render them more human."[124]

In this modern treatment Janssens attempts to meet head on the objections to his personalist method that have been raised.

latter article notes the importance of societal responsibility to the advancement of the individual. It is based on the tension between the objective and subjective culture, namely the call of the society to use what it has achieved to enhance the development of the persons within it. See pp. 13-15.

[120] "Personalist Morals," p. 14.

[121] This affirmation is not new in this article, however. See the much earlier treatment in "Moderne situatie-ethiek in het licht van de klassieke leer over het geweten," *Tijdschrift voor zielkunde en opvoedingsleer* 21 (1956) 172-198. In this earlier article he states: "Consequently all ethics is ultimately situation ethics: the moral life exists in responsible decision over concrete personal situations." ("Alle ethiek is dus uiteindelijk situatie-ethiek: het zedelijk leven bestaat in de verantwoordelijke beslissing over de koncrete, persoonlijke situaties."). See p. 73. Such statements as these, removed from their carefully nuanced context, have been the source of much negative reaction to Janssens' method.

[122] "Personalist Morals," p. 14.

[123] Cf. "Artificial Insemination: Ethical Considerations," pp. 10-11 (Theme 7).

[124] "Personalist Morals," p. 15.

We shall examine these objections later. Here we shall merely underline Janssens' final point, namely that the human person is essentially open to the supreme value, that is, God.[125] Janssens remains an optimist who trusts in the goodness of the responsive human person, one who is created as open to his/her creator. From this incarnate spirit one should hope and expect the best— choices that are benevolent and in keeping with the dignity of creatures imaged after a creator who is herself all goodness. This is the core of a Christian anthropology, as Janssens notes, which affirms the ultimate communion possible for humankind with God.

In sum, during this modern period Janssens has refined his thinking about norms as well as his thinking on the interface between the historical and spatial reality of human existence and morality (ontic evil). While the basic personalistic thrust has not changed, the way in which it is presented has become more refined, especially as Janssens attempts to respond both to the teaching of Vatican II and to those who do not accept or understand his method.

---

[125] The divine as an essential element of his method is consistent throughout Janssens' career. As he notes, " ... the religious element is fundamental. In every situation hides a call that God directs to us personally ... ." (" ... het religieus element is fundamental. In elke situatie schuilt een oproep die God tot ons persoonlijk ....") See "Modern situatie-ethick in het licht van de klassieke leer over het geweten," p. 75. It is precisely this divine element that distinguishes a Christian personalism from its counterparts. See chapter one.

CHAPTER THREE

AN ANALYSIS OF HIS VISION

His Philosophical Presuppositions

Personalism

To indicate that Janssens' moral methodology is personalist means first that it is rooted in the conscious, free, responsible human person, who functions as a moral subject. The person anchors Janssens' moral methodology as its primary value, thereby serving as morality's existential goal. From an existential perspective we can say that the human person lies at the starting point, the horizon, and the terminus of morality:

$$HP = value/ground/end$$

Personalism is not a unified system, but rather has taken many forms. Häring's summary outlined three basic types: 1) an I-thou personalism aimed at self perfection alone (the other used as means to achieve *my* value);[1] 2) a social form, in which the human person as a value is subjugated to the achievement of material perfection (Marx); 3) a radical I-thou personalism, in which the human person is perfected only in relationship, and especially in relationship to others like him/her self. Janssens, personalism is a clear illustration of this third type. Janssens cautions against using the other as a means (Type 1) or ranking the values of subjective culture beneath those of the objective culture (Type 2). Janssens' personalism illustrates a delicate balance between and among the various elements in the human

---

[1] Janssens comments, "True personal perfection ... has nothing in common with egoistic, self-enrichment based on the exploitation of others." "The Task of Today's State," *American College Bulletin* 34 (1955) 35.

relational system. To lose this balance is to destroy the meaning of his method. The human person never stands or functions alone but is always held in the tension of certain basic relationships. This is the second element in his method:

World ⟷ HP ⟷ Others

The human person interacts in a manner appropriate to his or her being-with the persons and things in the system. In this interaction self-fulfillment is achieved.

In addition, Janssens' personalism must be called a *Christian* personalism. This distinction further sets his method apart from the first two of Häring's types, since they concentrate either on the human person unrelated to a higher value or on the person as a function of the state. Even in his early patristic work Janssens demonstrates his grasp of the essential connection between the existence of the human person and a relationship with God. [2]

An understanding of his "love ethics" is key to understanding Janssens. On the human plane, love as a fundamental attitude of the person grounds human moral behavior. [3] Two things are necessary: first, the other is to be esteemed and valued as a

---

[2] It is interesting on this point to read Janssens' early patristic material. While his doctoral dissertation on divine filiation in Cyril of Alexandria has been lost, its content has been preserved to a large degree in the precís which appeared subsequently, "Notre filiation divine d'après saint Cyrille d'Alexandrie," *Ephemerides Theologicae Lovanienses* 15 (1938) 233-278. This work demonstrates Janssens' early fascination with the relationship between humanity and God. He notes that the mediation which Christ, the human-God, performs is physical. Human nature is reunited to divine nature in the unity of Christ's person. See p. 267. All people—good or evil—share a radical relationship (*parenté radicale*) with God. This relationship is raised to a higher level in the supernatural relationship that comes to believers through the Spirit of Christ. See pp. 275-276, for example. These ideas are not too far afield from those that we see developed in his later moral theology.

[3] The sequence of ideas used here is drawn in large part from Janssens' treatment as it appears in *Freedom of Conscience and Religious Freedom*, translated by Brother Lorenzo (Staten Island: Alba House, 1965) pp. 86-92.

person;[4] second, one must desire and seek the advancement and indeed the perfection of the other. As Janssens notes, "Certainly the end of our love is the person loved himself; but if the love is real, it desires that the person attain the perfection of which he is capable ...."[5]

Janssens expands this idea. In Christian revelation this philosophy of love is raised to a more explicit and higher plane. While the earthly teachings of Jesus call forth the best dimensions of humanity, they also underline the possibility of the incarnation of God's image in this world. Thus the "natural" law, which makes available to all certain first principles (in scholastic terms), sometimes called the "golden rule" (love others as oneself), is made explicit and thematic in the words and Word of revelation and subsequently in the actions of the believer. "Our openness to God means that we live in faith, hope and love."[6] This explicitation is precisely the Christian imitation of the love of Christ. In this categorical activity, scripture tells us, the Father becomes patent. The attitudes that inform this activity for the Christian are those found in "worship, prayer, contemplation, giving ourselves to God and putting ourselves at his disposal."[7] They become concrete in the real acts of Christians.[8]

---

[4] We have seen Janssens' extensive exposition of the concept of the "*even-naaste*," the other person as another self. See, for example, "Liefde en sociaal leven," p. 8, discussed above.

[5] *Freedom of Conscience and Religious Freedom*, p. 86. These two themes are nearly identical with the themes that Daniel Maguire uses to ground his social ethics. Maguire's "esteem and hope" correspond to Janssens' "esteem and desire for advancement." Cf. Daniel Maguire, "Personal and Social Ethics," (lecture), 7 March 1987, Cleveland, Ohio.

[6] "Artificial Insemination: Ethical Considerations," p. 9.

[7] "Norms and Priorities in a Love Ethics," p. 1.

[8] Note the dual end of these actions: on the one hand, as we emphasize here, the *result* is to make the love of God present; on the other hand, the *result* is to achieve the becoming of the person. Note further that these results are in some form of relationship with *attitudes*, which necessarily function to inform the intention of the agent. Cf. "Ontic Good and Evil: Premoral Values and Dis-values," pp. 62-63, for example. Below we shall examine the human action both from the perspective of the intention and the result in order to see precisely where the connection lies.

Janssens speaks of both an explicit motivation and an explicit content for Christian behavior. In postulating specific content Janssens appears to move beyond the neo-scholasticism that dominated the late nineteenth and early twentieth century, and to embrace a perspective which is more characteristic of the 1940's and 1950's. The post neo-scholastic period, according to MacNamara, attempted to supply the God dimension that was lacking in the neo-scholastic revival. It offered a new look at the scriptural tradition of *agape*, rooting the moral life in the love of God. Its tenets were three: 1) Christian morality presumed a life of grace in Christ, 2) charity is the organizing principle for Christian morality, 3) Christian moral life consists in an imitation of the life of Christ.[9]

While Janssens' work often seems to affirm a central place for the love of God and the categorical response of the Christian in imitation of Christ (and indeed sometimes refers to the specific command to love),[10] it moves more and more to locate God existentially and consequently ubiquitously. To locate the divine element in the real is to avoid the dualism that seems to result from an either/or approach: either morality is fully informed by life experience or it is found in the will of God as revealed concretely before human action. A look at Janssens' thinking as it develops through the years confirms a greater and greater appreciation of the real as God's point of contact with humanity.

With this development, a question must be raised. If God is able to be encountered in all reality, is there a uniqueness to the Christian content within reality? In earlier work Janssens appears to indicate that new content is involved.[11] In more recent work[12] the distinction is more blurred, as he speaks only of the ubiquitous presence of love as the source and criterion of human action.

[9] See Vincent MacNamara, *Faith and Ethics*: *Recent Roman Catholicism* (Washington: Georgetown University Press, 1985) pp. 14-36.

[10] See *Freedom of Conscience and Religious Freedom*, p. 87, for example.

[11] See, for example, the frankly Christian exposition in *Freedom of Conscience and Religious Freedom* , p. 87.

[12] See, for example, "Ontic Good and Evil: Premoral Values and Disvalues," *Louvain Studies* 12 (1987) 62

It is possible to conclude that Janssens' recent thinking is reflective of the movement in the 1970's which MacNamara terms a "groping towards autonomy."[13] This movement sees unique, or at least explicit, Christian motivation for action but no unique content. "... the religious realities—Christian truths—give a new significance and meaning to morality without changing its content .... There is ... an *extra* in Christian morality. But it is not primarily an ethical *extra*, rather a religious *extra*."[14]

Relationship with God in Christ results in freedom, pardon, and reconciliation for the person.[15] This freely given divine gift is in turn multiplied by the person in his/her behavior toward others. Revelation serves to illustrate this idea both formally and materially in the actions of Jesus. In turn human choice results in the epiphany of divine love in concrete human actions. In the existential realm of human self creation the series of categorical (individual, existential) acts done in this mode move the person closer and closer to his/her ultimate goal: union with God. Therefore God, who is love, is available as both the source and terminus of the human person. We may express, then, the third element in Janssens' method, the integral involvement of God:

$$HP \longleftrightarrow God$$

Finally, all the elements can be placed together in a complete schematic model. The model is personalistic, extended and bound in the real, and grounded in a reciprocity with the divine:

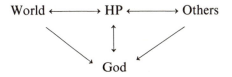

[13] See MacNamara, p. 39.

[14] MacNamara draws on Fuchs' work. See discussion, p. 42.

[15] *Freedom of Conscience and Religious Freedom*, pp. 87-88.

Existentialism

The second thing that can be said about Janssens' method is that it is existential. Perhaps we are not saying anything new here, since the personalism expressed above is clearly existential. This ontological point of departure is important to understanding Janssens, however. As Heidegger and those who adopted the thrust of his thinking do, Janssens grounds his method in the real. The starting point is always the person-in-being-there. Initially, the "there" can be defined by the set of enduring relationships of person with world and with others.

From another perspective, however, the "there" is the temporal and spatial plane of worldly existence. It has to do with activity and movement as well as with ontology. It is a set of changing relationships. To examine "there" in this sense, that is as consistent increments of change, is to begin to penetrate more deeply the meaning of the human person in Janssens' method and to focus on important implications for a teleological ethical system. In the expanse of time the human person (and the things and persons with which s/he interacts) is in a progressive journey along a continuum of points. These points are moments of history, both the history of the individual person and the history of the totality of humankind, since every living person moves simultaneously forward on the time continuum. I am encountered and described at point "A," and in that instant I have become present at point "B."[16] This definition in time and space describes at the same time both the "thereness" and the continual state of "not-thereness" that characterizes the human person.

[16] These ideas are better understood, perhaps, from the perspective of a process theology, which takes as its point of reference moments of time rather than pieces of matter. While no claim is made to a connection between Janssens and the process school, the temporal themes here are not incompatible. See, for example, Alfred North Whitehead, *Process and Reality* (New York: Macmillan, 1929); Charles Hartshorne, *The Divine Relativity: a Social Conception of God* (New Haven, CT: Yale University, 1948); Robert Mellert, *What Is Process Theology?* (New York: Paulist, 1975); and John B. Cobb, Jr., and David Ray Griffin, *Process Theology* (Philadelphia: Westminster, 1976).

Yet, as Janssens has pointed out, it is precisely in this movement through the incremental acts of choice in time that the human person becomes. "[W]e must perform our acts over different, successive moments of time."[17] The human person is *changing* in self and *changing* in situation at every moment of his/her existence. This change is the necessary activity that produces the definitive entity of who s/he is at any given point in the process. In addition, it is in the frame of concrete reality as it exists up to this point in history that persons discover objective values to be used as reference for the evaluation of moral action.[18] Because of the urgency of this becoming reality, though, at each point the person must leave behind some values unrealized, some "goods" unaccomplished.

The spatial aspect of the human person defines that person as bound to this place, because of the material enfleshment (incarnate spirit) which defines its being in reality. All activity of this concrete human entity is confined to the physical location in which s/he exists. Although I can imagine other places or see myself performing other tasks, in my body I can do this task only here and now. Further, the spatial world is where the free deeds of one person become "traversed" (*doorkruist*) or intersect with the free deeds of others.[19]

The implications of spatiality are several. First, the person must work through the body to relate to and have some effect on

[17] "Ontic Good and Evil: Premoral Values and Disvalues," p. 68. For English speaking readers Janssens' discussion and application of the implications of time and space in moral theology is known chiefly through his article, "Ontic Evil and Moral Evil" (1972) and its 1987 update. These ideas are, however rooted in a much earlier Janssens. As early as 1947 he was concerned with problems associated with time and space. See "Tijd en ruimte in de moraal," in *Miscellanea moralia*, BETL, 2 (Louvain: Nauwelaerts, 1947) pp. 181-197, now translated as "Time and Space in Morals" in Joseph A. Selling, ed., *Personalist Morals* (Louvain: University Press, 1988) pp. 9-22. See also "Geweten en zedelijke waarde," *Collationes Brugenses et Gandavenses* 12 (1966) 435.

[18] Further, it is in this frame that the human person is confronted with the inadequacy and imperfection of both the self and the environment. This world *manqué* is the basis for Janssens' thesis of ontic evil, treated below.

[19] "Time and Space in Morals," p. 20.

the world. This can result in the creation of real goods, which contribute to the development of the world. Second, the person is subject to the changeable nature of bodiliness. What Janssens calls the "burden of weariness" or illness and its effects or "the impact of the world"[20] catalogues in part the negative aspects of spatiality and points to the "fundamental ambiguity" of human life in its corporality.[21]

We must conclude that each aspect—temporal and spatial—is both enabling and limiting. In precisely the time and place that allows the categorical exercise of conscious, responsible, free action, I am bound to only certain choices and precluded, precisely because of these choices, from making others. Janssens notes that "every free act ... carries the consequences of my being limited."[22] Each commission is parent as well to an omission.[23] Further, in positing a certain action which results in a good, I find that some of the results—albeit often unforeseen—are evil.[24] Finally, my actions in time and space place me in essential involvement with the activities and free choices of other people.

Janssens has understood this paradox and has explored it carefully in his methodology. First, it is the basis for his description of objective and subjective culture. Objective culture, as we have seen, is precisely the pool of existent accomplishments of humankind to date. Its set includes technology, art, values, and so forth. As humankind travels collectively along the continuum of time, the set is enlarged by the discoveries and deposit within the culture of the new.[25] The ever increasing cultural pool serves

---

[20] "Ontic Good and Evil: Premoral Values and Disvalues," pp. 64-65.

[21] "Ontic Evil and Moral Evil," p. 135.

[22] "Time and Space in Morals," p. 20.

[23] See "Ontic Evil and Moral Evil," p. 134.

[24] Janssens is inclined in his writing to give pertinent examples of the points he is trying to make. He tells the homey story of a war time dilemma, for example, in which someone (the narrator of the story himself, it is presumed) sought the healthy result that comes from vigorous walking. The good consequence is offset, however, by the negative result of wearing out the leather of his shoes, scarce products during the second world war. (Interview with Louis Janssens, 29 April 1986, Louvain, Belgium.)

[25] It must be remembered that for Janssens this discovery is not merely human activity. It is rather response to the divine within creation.

as an ever growing point of reference for human moral activity. Janssens has contributed significantly to the understanding of moral theology merely by defining this phenomenon. Some of the major stumbling blocks in moral decision making stem from attempting to graft old answers onto new situations. By placing "new situations" in a positive existential context of human discovery and explicitation of God's world, another way of saying "growing objective culture," Janssens has framed a difficult problem in a context that makes it an interesting and conquerable challenge. We shall explore this idea more fully below, in the section dealing with norms.

Subjective culture likewise is the product of categorical choices, in this case of individual human persons who are creating something new for and in themselves. In the shaping of subjective culture the person is shaping him/her self as well. This is the essence of moral activity, the root of human behavior. Janssens' personalism is rooted in this value: the achievement of the unique subjective culture that is the extension and fulfillment of each human person.

Second, the spatial/temporal reality implies what Janssens calls ontic evil.[26] It is the categorical and contingent negation implied by the situation of living together with others in the world and in the sinful situation that humankind shares.[27] Ontic evil is the derivative of a world *manqué*. As Janssens puts it:

> The realities of this world are created and thus contingent and limited .... Whether these realities are good or evil, carriers of values or disvalues, depends upon their objective qualities toward which our intentional feelings are directed independently of our free will. The term morality is thus not applicable to these realities

[26] The term is Janssens'. The idea is found elsewhere, however, in Fuchs' "premoral evil" and Schüller's "non-moral evil" and the manuals' "physical evil," as McCormick notes. See Richard A. McCormick, *Notes on Moral Theology: 1965-1980* (Lanham, MD:UPA, 1981) p. 534.

[27] Cf. "Ontic Evil and Moral Evil," p.134; and "Ontic Good and Evil: Premoral Values and Disvalues," p. 63. In the more recent article Janssens condenses the category of "living with others in the world" into his "spatiality" discussion.

because only that which comes forth from a free decision (our interior attitude and our choice of concrete acts) [see discussion below] can be the object of a moral judgment.[28]

In other words, ontic evil is real evil that exists in the world that is not under the precise jurisdiction of the willing agent, but that has an impact on that agent or his/her actions. Another way of expressing this concept is the term "premoral disvalues."[29] The negative or evil aspects of reality exist in the field that presents itself in time before the subject, a part of the set of possibilites for action contained in the deliberation of a concrete moral choice. Sometimes the actualization of these possiblities is avoidable; sometimes it is not. We shall treat this aspect in greater detail below, when discussing the principle of the double effect. In this section it is sufficient to note the concept of ontic evil, particularly as it flows from the temporal and spatial condition, that is, the existential reality, of the human person.

There is a third area in which the existential situation affects the knowing, free, and responsible human person. Janssens has noted the connection between the temporal and spatial aspects of the person and the formation and exercise of conscience.[30] As Janssens points out in several places, conscience formation is the product of the early education by parents.[31] From the experience of love by his/her parents the child learns what is meant by relationship and what is expected in relationships of love. Displeasure by the mother, for example, gives the child an experience of relationship broken before a thematized understanding of what this means is developed. This is the prelude or prologue (*voorspel*)

[28] "Ontic Good and Evil: Premoral Values and Disvalues," p.80.

[29] Ibid., p. 81.

[30] The full implications of conscience in Janssens' method will be addressed later. In this section it is our intention merely to underline the relationship of conscience to the existential position of the human person.

[31] Generally Janssens' work presupposes the value of a traditional model of a two-parent family, although he is not blind to the influences of the modern world on family life (see discussion of these changes in "Christendom en geweten," *De gids op maatschappelijk gebied* 49 [1958] 891-894).

of conscience.[32] The generous love and support of the parent, from whom the child receives certain rules of behavior, is replaced in mature life by an understanding of the love of God as the font of morality.[33] This love is the condition for the formation of conscience. Thus the adult, grounded and motivated in love, is able to choose wisely and morally. The formation of conscience depends on the adequate appropriate input from close relational situations over time. If these early series of experiences are deprived or lacking in any way, the person comes to adulthood unwhole, unable to exercise conscience perfectly.

The second way in which the temporal and spatial affect the person's exercise of conscience has already been indicated above. If my knowledge is incomplete—as it must certainly be because of my existential limits—I am not completely free in my choice of the total moral good.[34] My moral judgment regarding the efficacy of any concrete action is affected by the limitations of the concrete situation. Therefore, on the existential (not necessarily the moral) plane it is always incomplete and fallible in at least some aspects. Indeed, this is another example of the presence of ontic evil in one's environment and of the tension between the ideal and the real. As Janssens put it:

> Indeed our knowledge of truth is defective. We can only consider one aspect of reality at a time. We will never exhaust the richness of truth. Although we do not possess truth, we are constantly searching for it. This implies that our knowledge is subject to the limitations of ignorance.... certain aspects of norms and situations can elude us and we err in synthesizing the elements of our

[32] See "Christendom en geweten," p. 897-890.

[33] In one of Janssens' more extensive treatments of conscience formation he notes the stages that inform adult moral decision making by the judgment of conscience: 1) love and affection from parents; 2) models of good conscience drawn from actual people or from stories (biblical pericopes, for example); 3) an ongoing process of self reflection on the motives for action. See "Gewetensvorming," in *God is groter: werkboek rond het geloven*, 3rd ed. (Lannoo: Tielt-Weesp, 1985) pp. 453-454.

[34] See "The Foundation for Freedom of Conscience," *American College Bulletin* 43 (1964) 17, where Janssens notes that good will alone is insufficient to force complete freedom from error in a concrete situation.

perspective knowledge which is thus spatial. Subjected thus to the limitations of ignorance, and by that very fact to the deficiencies wrought by error, we continually run the risk of forming erroneous judgments of conscience in good faith.[35]

Neo-scholasticism

Janssens' thinking has also been influenced by the return to Thomistic thought, associated with scholastic revival of the early twentieth century. His work exhibits in particular a devotion to the authentic insights of Thomas (as evidenced by his numerous references to the Dominican thinker).[36] In *Personne et société* there is to be found the distinction that Maritain makes between the individual and the person.[37] Janssens espouses the natural law theory, which locates the source of moral wisdom within the created world for rational humankind to discover. Janssens reflects the neo-scholasticism that moved beyond the safety of "strict observance Thomism"[38] into new areas. In Janssens' work it is evident that he has not been content merely to rehash what had been done already, but he has sought to recover the "real" Thomas Aquinas and to ground much of his own original thinking on that recovery.

The basis of the moral methodology used by Thomas Aquinas was an Aristotelian philosophy, which examined causality: formal, efficient, material, final. For Thomas, however, *the* important factor in causation was God. In a classical world view God was seen as the beginning and the end of morality. No distinction needed to be made, then, between a deontological approach, which focused on pre-existent norms, and a teleological approach, which sought the proper end as moral, since in fact

[35] "The Foundation for Freedom of Conscience," p. 19. Cf. "Geweten en zedelijke waarde," p. 453.

[36] Jans has noted that Janssens is never far from his copy of Thomas' *Summa*. Indeed it is rumored that he keeps it at his bedside for quick reference. Interview with Jan Jans, 30 April 1986, Louvain, Belgium.

[37] See chapter one, p. 19.

[38] See chapter one, p. 19.

these were identical. An insight into this approach, appropriated in much of the neo-scholastic renewal, is gained by the following from MacNamara:

> What strikes one immediately about almost all the manuals is that the whole treatment of morality is dominated by a short introductory section on the last end of the human person. God, the neo-Scholastic said, created us for a purpose—the purpose of union with him in heaven. Our business on earth is to achieve that purpose. Morality falls into place as the way or the means to that end.[39]

He goes on to say that the neo-scholastics look to law, ultimately given humankind by God, who is in charge of the world, to uncover what is moral. Further, morality is conceived as actualizing "the law of God, his eternal law."[40] There is a clear connection between the law, preceding the act, and the end. A glitch in this well-oiled system occurred, however, when a different world view was espoused. If all wisdom were not contained in a pre-existing set of norms that were congruent with an actualization in some final effect; if there really was newness, the "teleological" (read: "deontological") system appropriated by the neo-Thomists would need adjustment. Indeed, Janssens' method reflects this adjustment. To fully comprehend Janssens, then, we must examine in greater detail a modern approach to the distinction between deontology and teleology. This we shall do in the following section.

Situating Janssens' Method

Since moral theology in the United States has become an increasingly ecumenical discipline, a significant number of American Catholic moralists have tried to render the wealth of Roman Catholic theological tradition in a common philosophical lan-

[39] MacNamara, p. 10.
[40] Ibid.

guage,[41] one which can relate more adequately to other traditions. Janssens' ideas, although cited with some frequency in this analysis,[42] have not been understood by everyone who invokes his name.[43] A clarification of the terminology wil prove useful, as will its appropriate application to Janssens. His valuable insights have much to offer in the debate.

Discussions in moral theology in the last several decades frequently have borrowed constructs from philosophy to describe ethical theories. C. D. Broad, in a seminal book *Five Types of Ethical Theory*,[44] was the first to establish the terms "deontology" and "teleology" to refer to opposing philosophies of normative ethics.[45] His contrasting pair have travelled through the decades, sometimes understood, sometimes altered, but generally useful in discerning the perspective of philosophers and theologians in the panorama of moral discourse. As Baier's preface to his discussion on the topic points out, dichotomies can serve to organize positions of disagreement from their originating insight or stance.[46] The deontology/teleology debate provides a focal question: is ethics supposed to be based on duty or consequences?

[41] Lisa Cahill, for example, cites "a general and considerable unclarity in recent ethical literature about the conceptual tools of moral philosophy and modes of argument in moral theology." See "Teleology, Utilitarianism, and Christian Ethics," *TS* 42 (1981) 601.

[42] See, for example Cahill, pp. 607 and 611; McCormick, *Notes on Moral Theology: 1965-1980*, pp. 760-761; and Gula, pp. 69-74.

[43] See, for example, Paul M. Quay, "The Disvalue of Ontic Evil," *TS* 46 (1985) 262-286. This rather pointed attack on Janssens' work, especially the 1972 article on ontic evil, have been answered by Janssens in his recent article "Ontic Good and Evil: Premoral Values and Disvalues," *Louvain Studies* 12 (1987) 62-82.

[44] C. D. Broad, *Five Types of Ethical Theory* (London: Routledge and Kegan Paul, 1930).

[45] Lisa Cahill makes this observation, p. 602; as does Connery, p. 261, n. 2. Cf. Bruno Schüller, "Various Types of Grounding for Ethical Norms," *Readings 1*, pp. 184-185. This article appeared originally in German "Typen der Begründung sittlicher Normen," *Concilium* 120 (1976) 648-654.

[46] Kurt Baier, "Ethics: Deontological Theories," in Warren T. Reich, ed., *Encyclopedia of Bioethics*, (New York: Free Press, 1978) p. 413. Baier's discussion of the opposing theories is most helpful. See also "Ethics: Teleological Theories," pp. 417-421.

Previous attempts have been made to situate Louis Janssens' position in relationship to these categories. The editorial comment at the beginning of one of his major articles in 1977 casts Janssens as a deontologist.[47] Today his name appears most frequently among those referred to as mixed consequentialists or revisionists.[48] It will be helpful, therefore, to see which, if any, of these categorical shoes fits.

The focus of discussion on the poles of ethical theory has been important recently in Roman Catholic circles. Catholic moral theology is based on God's revelation to humankind, not only in the person of Jesus Christ and the written symbolization of the good news in scripture, but also as this revelation is part of the historical development of the church. Some would understand that God speaks explicitly and precisely through the institutional church in such a way as to make human analysis and reason irrelevant (ecclesiastical positivism). Further, they understand this divine word as absolute and therefore constantly valid. Thus the divine will can be expressed in concrete norms, which, when proclaimed by the magisterium,[49] become imperatives for human activity.[50]

Modern technology (raising new moral questions to be addres-

---

[47] See the brief introduction to "Norms and Priorities in a Love Ethics," *Louvain Studies* 6 (1977) 207. Certainly Janssens' devotion to Roman Catholic tradition and his conservative—in the best sense of the word—approach to norms places him within the company of many who merit this description. The editor of the journal claims, however, that the term was a *lapsus calami*. His intention was to type Janssens as a teleologist.

[48] See, for example, Gula, p. 69.

[49] This term is generally used to denote the teaching authority of the church, whose function is to sustain in history a clear witness to the revelation in Jesus Christ. For a more extensive treatment see Francis A. Sullivan, *Magisterium: Teaching Authority in the Catholic Church* (Mahwah: Paulist, 1983); Charles E. Curran and Richard A. McCormick, eds. *Readings in Moral Theology No. 3: The Magisterium and Morality* (New York: Paulist, 1982); and Avery Dulles, *A Church to Believe In* (New York: Crossroad, 1982), especially chapters seven and eight.

[50] Certain areas apt for moral consideration have received more attention in this matter than others. Questions dealing with human life and those concerned with sexual activity are particularly singled out, for example. Louis Janssens' work comes into conflict with past thinking in precisely such sensitive areas, as we shall see.

sed) and modern thinking (encouraged in the Catholic world, no doubt, by the emphasis at Vatican II on religious and decision making freedom) have, however challenged such a perspective. Consequently Catholic moral theologians of different, sometimes conflicting, positions have become involved in a complementary and critical process to evaluate behavior and to establish terminology in which to frame such dialogue. The Catholic natural law tradition, too, has been mined for insight in this discussion.

Although the flurry of articles on deontology, teleology, and so forth, has waned in Europe (Janssens himself does not see the question as significant), this is not the case in America, where philosophers and theologians alike have taken up the discussion. Perhaps fueled by the emergence of new problems in the field of medical ethics which seem to demand a clarification of methodology, many American Catholic moral theologians are still interested in situating the debate.[51] Further, moral theology has become in this country an increasingly ecumenical discipline.[52] The philosophical language established by Broad provides a common tongue for discussion among those familiar with Roman Catholic tradition and those from other backgrounds.

In Broad's original categories deontology was defined as ethical

[50a] See below, chapter four.

[51] Such prominent Roman Catholic theologians as Charles Curran and Richard McCormick have not found the topic meaningless. See, for example Curran's article on "Utilitarianism and Contemporary Moral Theology: Situating the Debate," which appeared in *Louvain Studies* 6 (1976-77) 239-255, and which has been included in his *Themes in Fundamental Moral Theology* (Notre Dame: University Press, 1977) and its updated version *Directions in Fundamental Moral Theology* (Notre Dame: University Press, 1985). McCormick often has referred to the distinction in his annual March contributions to *Theological Studies*. Gula likewise addresses the question at some length, as does Baier in his contribution to the *Encyclopedia of Bioethics*.

[52] See, for example, the list of contributions in the field of medical ethics alone provided in David Kelly's book, cited above, p. XI, n. 4. Some Protestant moral theologians have taken up the traditional Catholic positions with such vigor that it is impossible to categorize them without a denominational scorecard. I offer, for example, Paul Ramsey, whose positions often echo the strongest themes found in the history of Roman moral song.

theory that holds certain actions to be right (or wrong) in such and such circumstances, no matter what the consequences.[53] Teleological theories tie rightness or wrongness to the realization of certain consequences which are themselves good or bad.[54] At the onset these definitions appear fairly patent.[55] Most of those who cite Broad are quite content with them. It is important to go deeper, however, if we are to understand them in relationship to Janssens' moral methodology.

First, with regard to deontological theories, Broad notes that there is an element of teleological thrust to them. His deontologist takes no account of the *goodness* or *badness* of intended consequences, as does his model teleologist, but does evaluate the consequence(s) directly connected with conformity with the formal statement safeguarded in the norm (duty to follow norm). Therefore s/he is concerned with the rightness or wrongness of the consequences in congruence with that norm.[56] Thus for the deontologist "a lie is wrong simply and solely because it is

[53] The origin of the word, however, is to be found in work of the famous utilitarian, Jeremy Bentham. This is pointed out in Baier, p. 413; and in Cahill, p. 602.

[54] Broad, pp. 206-207. Interestingly, Broad provides insight into some of the knotty critique aimed at McCormick and others as having to prioritize values in determining consequences by his further discussion of monistic and pluralistic theories. He notes as well that some theories that appear to be deontological are, in fact, teleological, since they derive their deontological principles from teleological considerations. See especially p. 208.

[55] For clarity this discussion will be based on and limited to the definitions which Broad offers. Modern understanding of the various terms used in the debate sometimes is confused, since different authors may use such terms as "utilitarian," "consequential," "teleological," and "proportional" in a variety of ways. See, for example, Finnis' attempt to clarify, pp. 80-86. I would venture to say that much of the disagreement among moralists can be traced to semantic problems with each others' positions.

[56] Frankena further differentiates between the rule-deontologist, who conforms to basic judgments of obligation, e.g., "We ought always to keep our promises," and the act-deontologist, whose obligation or duty derives from the unique situation, e.g., "In this situation I should do so and so." In both instances, however, the duty is derived without appeal to the production of good over evil in the consequences or to any value that might be actualized, except the value of acting in conformity to the recognized obligation. William K. Frankena, *Ethics* (Englewood Cliffs: Prentice-Hall, Incorporated, 1963), especially pp. 14-15.

intended to produce a *false* belief, and not because a false belief is an intrinsically bad state of mind."[57] No further evaluation of consequences need be addressed. Note here the focus placed on the intention of the agent, however.

On the other hand the teleologist, says Broad, is concerned only with the goodness and badness of intended and relevant consequences. States Broad, "For the Teleologist the other characteristics of the consequences are relevant only in so far as they make the consequences intrinsically *good* or *bad*, and to say that a lie is wrong simply means that its consequences will on the whole be bad."[58] Contained in this idea, I think, is the notion of ontic good and ontic evil, to employ terms defined after Broad. Broad's teleologist judges actions moral or immoral based on his or her evaluation of the relative ontic good or evil produced by the action. The agent's action is largely empirical: to ascertain in this setting the good or evil that will flow from the anticipated action.

Yet, as Broad points out, there is at least one *a priori* consideration: there are certain forms which, existent, are already judged to embody good (or, one would assume, evil). These ideas provide the agent with a pre-existing set of goods or values which may serve as referent in the decision making process. How can one evaluate the good or evil of consequences if one has no notion of what constitutes good or evil?[59] Broad touches here something of importance that is often neglected in the deontological-teleological discussion, namely the dependence of the elements of one pole of the theory on the other pole.

In order to evaluate consequences it would seem that the teleologist must take into account the entire spectrum of possible consequences. In fact, this question is often raised by those who criticize the so-called revisionists (among whom Janssens is often

[57] Broad, p. 209.

[58] Ibid.

[59] I would point out that Broad steers clear of a purely quantitative evaluation of conseqeunces. For him the bottom line is more than a cost-benefit survey. Indeed, most modern so-called "utlilitarians" do not espouse what Finnis calls hedonistic and eudaemonistic utilitarian theories, but rather use more inclusive categories. See p. 81.

included) as being unable to evaluate such a widespread field. Broad's response is that the teleologist must take into account those consequences which the agent has intended and "which the agent foresaw and desired or tolerated."[60] Implicit in this statement is the reality that no agent can foresee every consequence which flows from a particular action. It is sufficient, therefore, to assess reasonably what one can and to intend that. Note again the moral weight of the agent's intention here. Broad sees that the problems of limited vision intrude in the working of the deontologist as well. The deontologist deals with the problem, however, simply by limiting the range of consideration to

> certain characteristics of a certain restricted part of its total intended consequences. If, *e.g.*, its immediate consequences had a certain characteristic, then it would be right (or wrong) no matter what might be its remoter consequences and no matter what might be the other characteristics of its immediate consequences.[61]

Therefore more remote consequences which may not embody congruence with the perceived duty are excluded from the discussion. One key to differentiating the two theories and to applying them to Janssens lies in the function and direction of the intention of the agent. For the deontologist the intention of the agent is to seek conformity to the duty, perceived as a universal maxim that goes before the action of the agent as a kind of pattern for behavior. The roots of this duty are found in universal normative statements, for example, God's command (rule-deontologists) or in a clear perception arising from the concrete situation (act-deontologists). In both cases there is a non-existential and pre-determining component to it: the intention moves, in a sense, backward toward congruence with that component.

The teleologist, on the other hand, moves forward in intention. S/he attempts to conform to the good perceived as possibility for the future as the basis for action. Therefore the teleologist is always grounded in the real, the existential horizon of his or her

---

[60] Broad, p. 211.
[61] Broad, p. 212.

activity. While there is the *a priori* consideration of what constitutes the good, the movement of the intention is in conformity to its object, which when acted upon will actualize the pre-moral value seen as the good.[62]

Perhaps it would be helpful here to clarify these ideas by means of a diagram:

A pure teleological model:

Agent conforms intention to

$$\frac{good}{evil} \text{ consequences } = \text{ morally good act}$$

a priori consideration: what constitutes good?
direction of movement: toward the future

A pure deontological model:

Agent conforms intention to
    duty = morally good act
a priori consideration: what constitutes right?
direction of movement: toward the past

It may be helpful here to demonstrate the modern Roman Catholic intersection with these ideas. Catholic tradition had formerly assumed an often monolithic position congruent with the deontology described above. If God is the creator of the world and if God's providence is constantly and definitely active in the things of the world, there may be certain actions or categories of actions which are always a matter of duty or always a matter of action to be avoided, since they reflect God's plan. Conclusions from this thesis have been made explicit in certain

---

[62] Vacek makes a similar point about the directional movement of deontology and teleology. See Edward V. Vacek, "Proportionalism: One View of the Debate," *TS* 46 (1985) 292.

teachings of the church.[63] Underlying this position is the tacit assumption that the world and human beings are unchangeable. Says Gula:

> This classicist world view works on the assumption that the world is a finished product. Everything is done; nothing new is to be added .... One only needs to look upon the world to discover its order. A good look grasps immutable essences which yield a high degree of certitude and can be stored up to remain valid forever.[64]

It is easy to see how such a position would tend to define some activities as always evil. If things do not change, it is clear that what is right or wrong can be predetermined and specified. If one formulates norms built on this perception, and further, sees such norms as rooted or originating in God's law, it would follow that there is no dispensation from them since they can never be in error.

The third category of ethical theory is one that initially appears to be a modern midrash on the two theories outlined in Broad's work. Indeed it is an attempt to mediate the problems inherent in a deontological position with a world view that no longer accepts a static pre-digested universe. Gula's definition is helpful here. He indicates that the revisionist or mixed consequentialist position refers to "those Catholic theologians who are rooted in the Catholic tradition, acknowledge its achievements, but are modifying the classical language and method of that tradition."[65]

The position demonstrates a turn from the strongly deontological thrust of Catholic moral theology that characterized the period of the manuals and which was practically synonymous with the pre-Vatican II church. This position assumed as unchangeable and given certain moral absolutes. These moral absolutes found their source in the natural law or in the teaching authority of the church.

Curran and others have pointed out in abundant detail the two

---

[63] Specific applications have been made in cases dealing with the presumed fixed nature of humanity, for example. See below, chapter four.

[64] Gula, p. 18.

[65] Ibid., p. 51, n. 34.

interpretations of natural law that have existed in the church. On the one hand natural law is seen as the tendency of human reason to seek the true and of human will to move toward the good (metaethical level). The other approach to natural law emphasizes a biological teleology and has been evoked primarily in dealing with matters pertinent to sexuality (normative level). To elect to act in violation of such natural law is, in a classicist world view, to elect that which is intrinsically evil, since it violates what is a participation in the immutable eternal law of God (metaethical *and* normative level come together).[66] Modern moral theologians who espouse this theory can be called deontologists.[67] Those who deny the existence of any intrinsically evil acts or categories are generally designated consequentualists.

The revisionist modification, according to Gula, consists in looking to pre-moral values as referents in moral decision making, since they articulate "the basic goods which define the human possibility for growth."[68] While this seems initially to imitate Grisez's deontological position, the method by which it is worked out is different. Here the options which best actualize these basic goods are those which are ultimately to be chosen as morally praiseworthy. While there are certain pre-moral values articulated, they have no weight or meaning which overrides the consideration of the real situation. The choice is found in the judgment of the proportion of good over evil, or, to quote Gula again, "If there is no value proportionate to the disvalue produced, then the action is morally evil."[69]

Curran offers three points which constitute his version of mixed consequentialism: "(1) moral obligation arises from elements other than consequences [presumably the same idea as Gula's

---

[66] See, for example, Curran, *Directions in Fundamental Moral Theology* (Notre Dame: University Press, 1985) pp. 119-131; Gula, pp. 34-44.

[67] As Gula notes, "In a deontological approach the norm becomes the principal reference by which actions are judged to be morally right or wrong" (p. 81).

[68] Gula, p. 79.

[69] Ibid., p. 81.

pre-moral values consideration], (2) the good is not separate from the right [the evaluation of what is good is informed by objective considerations], (3) the way in which the good or evil is achieved by the agent is a moral consideration [since Gula's treatment concentrates on norms, a consideration of the agent is less pertinent]."[70] Curran's schema is an obvious direct answer to the objections which he claims deontologists raise vis-à-vis consequentialism.[71]

It seems to me that Curran's lengthy definition of mixed consequentialism comes remarkably close to many modern definitions of deontology.[72] Perhaps this is due to the fact that *both* deontology and teleology use elements that precede and follow the activity of the agent. The key is found in how these elements are used. In both theories the right and the good interact; indeed, there is an almost circular dynamic to the distinction. In teleology, it is the *good* that determines the *right*.[73] Therefore action that is praiseworthy is determined to some extent existentially. In deontology, it is the *right* that determines the *good*. Therefore action that is praiseworthy is that which conforms, at least in some aspects, to something other than an evaluation of what is actualized, that is existential considerations.

It is precisely the consideration of the existential that provides the key to understand why the question of ethical categories is so decisive in modern Roman Catholic moral theology. The preoccupation by some Catholic moral theologians with these distinctions is explained by what they assess as the pressing need to find a viable marriage between a changed worldview, which champions a developmental approach to life and questions the

[70] Charles E. Curran, *Directions in Fundamental Moral Theology*, p. 185.

[71] Cf. p. 180.

[72] I am not alone in this perception. See Richard McCormick's discussion on the topic, *Notes on Moral Theology: 1965-1980*, pp. 650 651 especially. McCormick, in examination of several theologians' work, accents the difficulty in a having a variety of approaches to the subject.

[73] See J. C. C. Smart and Bernard Williams, *Utilitarianism: For or Against* (Cambridge: University Press, 1973) p. 118.

existence of a set of static givens,[74] and a religious tradition which holds that the revelation in Jesus Christ and the establishment of the church are givens which are not negotiable.

Supported by a clearer understanding of Broad's original categories and this clarification of the way in which the two theories operate, I suggest that so-called mixed consequentialism is merely a recovery of the original teleological category as outlined by Broad and does not really constitute a new model. The trick is to understand and accept the deontological *elements* that are and always were present in the category. This is precisely what Curran and others who represent the same position do. This model provides a method for Catholic thinking to conserve the values inherent in the tradition in a workable method that is existentially rooted.[75] As indicated above, Broad's definitions often are not examined carefully. On the other hand the illusion that mixed consequentialism is merely a "new deontology," as Curran's model seems initially to imply,[76] is explained by an imprecise understanding of the terms "right" and "good"[77] and where they fit in the respective theories.

The remaining problem—mercifully outside the scope of the present endeavor, but left to those proficient in the rarer atmospheres of ethics—is to ascertain how one grounds the *a priori*

[74] See, for example, Vacek, p. 294. He calls for a methodology that "takes historicity seriously."

[75] It may be obvious to students of Thomas Aquinas that the new mixed consequentialism is perhaps a rediscovery of the wheel that Thomas provided with his methodology which rolled well for centuries. This connection did not go unheeded in Janssens' work.

[76] Cf. pp. 180 and 185. Curran's "middle position" seems to be molded exactly from the deontological objections to utilitarianism, teleology, and consequentialism. The objections themselves appear to me to outline rather well the deontological position.

[77] The terms are used here in this sense: right and wrong refer to the ought questions, those which relate to criteria and standards of behavior on the objective level of normative ethics. See John Ladd, "The Task of Ethics," *Encyclopedia of Bioethics*, pp. 403-404; and Smart and Williams, p. 13. Good and bad can be used to refer to evaluations of states of affairs or consequences. As such, these terms have implications for evaluating the subjective components (blame and praise) of morality. For further clarification, see n. 91 and chapter four, below.

considerations. The present problem, however, is to discover where Janssens fits in.

I suggest that Janssens is a teleologist in the Broad sense—if the reader will forgive an irresistible pun—of the word. As we shall see in greater detail in the following section, Janssens' moral method seeks to conform the intention and activity of the human agent to "the person adequately considered."[78] While this criterion, which articulates the notion of right, precedes the action of the agent, its contents (good/evil actualized) are available and evaluated only in the consequences. Janssens' method demands a congruence between the intention and the end, and the end implies the achievement of consequences.[79] The elaboration of precisely how this comes together is the work of the next section. The conclusion that must be drawn here in answer to the question of where Janssens fits is that he is a teleologist. This conclusion seems congruent with his method as far as we have seen it and is true to the Thomistic flavor that dominates his work.

The Human Person and the Moral Act

The body of science we call moral theology is fashioned upon a skeleton of terms. How one defines, juxtaposes, and grounds these terms determines the genus, and often the genius, of a particular moral method. We have considered already the grounding of Janssens' moral method in personalism and in various other philosophical systems. We have concluded that Janssens is a teleologist. Now we will look closely at the elements of the method themselves in order to understand what this means. The

---

[78] This phrase is found again and again in Janssens' work.

[79] We must likewise lay aside for the moment the question of how one defines the human person adequately considered. As Philip Keane has pointed out, this is a difficult task, given the nature of the human person: never fully able to catch up with self. See "The Objective Moral Order: Reflections on Recent Research," *TS* 43 (1982) 262.

questions we shall address are: 1) What constitutes the moral act? 2) What constitutes the right, or what criteria are used for evaluation of morality beyond the acting agent? 3) What is the relationship, and hence the moral implication, between the subjective and objective components?

The Moral Act: Seeking the Good

For Janssens, "morality is chiefly concerned with the human relationships and the well-being of human beings."[80] This element, the human person as focal point, is key. Morality exists in the subject, as it "only refers to our dispositions or attitude and to our actions."[81] Janssens locates the good (the existential element) as flowing from the person, acting in freedom and knowledge. An analysis of his approach to the moral act will illustrate this point. In his 1972 article "Ontic Evil and Moral Evil,"[82] Janssens examines the moral act in great detail vis-à-vis the thinking of Thomas Aquinas.[83] Following the scholastic doctor Janssens describes three components to be considered: 1) the *voluntas*, 2) the *intentio* and *electio*, 3) the *actus exterior*.[84]

The first component, *voluntas*, indicates the orientation of the will toward the good.[85] This orientation is a potency, a proper

[80] "Ontic Evil and Moral Evil," *Louvain Studies* 4 (1972) 139.

[81] "Norms and Priorities in a Love Ethics" p. 211. The English version of one of Janssens' primary articles is an expansion of "De zedelijke normen," *Ethische vragen voor onze tijd: hulde aan Mgr. Victor Heylen* (Antwerp: De Nederlandse Boekhandel, 1977) 37-58. The following year a structurally superior translation of the English article was published in Dutch, "Normen en prioriteiten in een ethiek van de liefde," *Sacerdos* 46 (1978-9) 15-31; 129-150. Cf. "Artificial Insemination: Ethical Considerations," p. 15. Cf. "Recht en moraal," p. 528. Cf. "Perspectives and Implications of Some Arguments of Saint Thomas," *ETL* 63 (1987) 354-360, p. 35.

[82] *Louvain Studies* 4 (1972-73) 115-156.

[83] The text used throughout the article is *De Actibus Humanis*, I, II, qq. 6-17.

[84] Janssens has described these components in earlier work. See *Personalisme en democratisering*, p. 69, for example. The discussion in the book lacks the painstaking attention to detail and references to Aquinas, but the content is substantially the same.

[85] See also, *Personne et société*, pp. 233-235, pp. 52-54. Janssens' thinking is never too far afield from Thomistic thinking. Rather, he tends to clarify some of

capacity, a predisposition to any actualization in a categorical act.[86] The "will strives for the end itself [the good] in an absolute way ... even if it is not connected with an action."[87] Notice that for Janssens this orientation and the perception of what constitutes the good are located and understood *within* the person;[88] hence we are presented with a frankly personalist methodology.

The second component, *intentio* and *electio*, indicates the fixing of the agent's intention or willing on a particular end and the correlative activity, the election of the means. Janssens (drawing on his own reading of Thomas) finds a necessary connection between these two aspects of the human act. In choosing a concrete object as the terminus of the act of the will the acting person is choosing the means that are appropriate and necessary to the attainment of that end. Further, it is the end intended by the subject that determines which means s/he elects. "Or, in other words, the sense of means can be attributed only to something from the point of view of the end: *ex fine enim oportet accipere rationes eorum quae sunt ad finem.*"[89] Janssens is most careful here in his presentation and in his reference to Thomas:

the insights from scholasticism that had been misinterpreted in the earlier twentieth century.

[86] "Ontic Evil and Moral Evil," pp. 118-119. This theme is examined in other places as well. See "Saint Thomas Aquinas and the Question of Proportionality," *Louvain Studies* 9 (1982-83) 42. Cf. "Moderne situatie-ethiek in het licht van de klassieke leer over het geweten," p. 83, in which Janssens discusses this orientation in its relationship to prudence. In the more recent article, "Ontic Good and Evil: Premoral Values and Disvalues," Janssens identifies this capacity or orientation with the motivating love (*benevolentia*) which Augustine saw as the essential predisposing element in human moral activity. Janssens situates love as the major element in the development of conscience as well. See "Geweten en zedelijke," p. 455, for example.

[87] "Ontic Evil and Moral Evil," pp. 118-119. Janssens assumes a (metaethical) natural law stance. See chapter four.

[88] He states, "The proper object of our will is the good *as it is apprehended* [emphasis mine] through our knowledge." "Perspectives and Implications of Some Arguments of Saint Thomas," p. 7.

[89] "Ontic Evil and Moral Evil," p. 119. In this section and below Janssens quotes from *De Actibus Humanis* of Thomas Aquinas. His citations are from I, II, q. 1, introduction and art. 3; q. 8, art. 3 ad. 1; and q. 12, art. 4 ad 3.

"The *intentio* is the striving toward the *end* to the extent that it is within the range of the *means*." "The *electio* is the concentration of the will on the *means* to the extent that they bear upon the attainment of the *end*." The material sense of both concepts is the same since they contain the idea of the whole act, end and means. But they are formally quite distinct. The *intentio* is directly aimed at the absolute element of the structure of the action, that is, the end itself which is the reason that the means are willed and consequently it is the principle of the act (*finis* as *principium actionis humanae*), the formal element which specifies the act. On the other hand, the *electio* signifies the relative [material] elements of the act, viz., the means (by its own definition means indicates a relation to the end) which is only useful until the end has been attained (*finis* as *terminus actionis humanae*).[90]

Therefore the end and the means are linked in an absolute manner in any concrete action. There are no means operative in *this* concrete act except those which function to produce *this* intended end.[91] For Janssens (and for Thomas in Janssens' reading) the human will embraces both terms in a single act:

$$\text{will} \xrightarrow{\text{embraces}} \text{(means and end)}$$

Further, it is the end which determines *which* means will be elected, since there must be a harmony of proportion[92] between the end and how it is achieved. Not just any means is appropriate to a particular end.

$$\text{will} \longrightarrow \quad \text{(means} \xleftarrow{\text{determines}} \text{end)}$$

[90] "Ontic Evil and Moral Evil," p. 119.

[91] The subject may or may not be presented with a broad set of means among which to choose in a given instance. I suggest that a paucity of means available in a given situation will have a tendency to limit the freedom of the moral agent and to increase the possibility of ontic evil which flows from the particular act.

[92] We shall look at this component in greater detail below.

The moral significance of human action, then, is constituted and determined by the congruence in these elements. It is a congruence between the intention of the subject and the object (includes means and end) toward which the agent aims:

$$\text{intention} \longleftrightarrow \text{object}$$

The third component of the moral action is the *actus exterior*, the real event or consequence that results from the above process. Janssens has made the point again and again that intentions must be actualized in real deeds, in categorical realities in time and space. It is only in this context that they can be perceived or have impact on either the becoming subject or on the rest of reality. "The action must be *done* in order to effect the end. To act is to be actively in touch with reality ...."[93] This "real event" does not designate only a material reality, however, but includes the inner act of the will (which, we remember, takes in the end and the means).[94] "Only the object defined in this way can have moral meaning ...   ."[95]

In sum, the moral act as it is unfolded in Janssens' method begins in the subject, is focused according to the purpose of the subject, and is completed in such a manner that it achieves the subjective intended result in an exterior event. The movement of the activity is concerned with what is to be, rather than what has been in the past. In its totality the moral act exhibits two things: 1) it is concerned primarily with the intention and action of the subject, that is, the person; 2) the movement of the act is always in terms of the future (that is, end and object) where the evaluation of the good is ultimately made. In a sense, the final object embraces the intention and the end (and thereby the means) of the acting person.

[93] "Ontic Evil and Moral Evil, p. 120.

[94] Ibid., p. 120; and "St. Thomas Aquinas and the Question of Proportionality," *Louvain Studies* 10 (1982-83) 37, 43.

[95] "St. Thomas Aquinas and the Question of Proportionality," p. 37.

Evaluation of the Right

So far Janssens may appear to make the evaluation of the good in a totally subjective manner. This is not the case. There are morally significant components in the method that reside, at least in some sense, outside the person. The nature of the exterior act which flows from the intention and action of the subject is far from irrelevant to moral evaluation. In a teleological system, the realized good in all its implications is the standard of morality. It is essential that the exterior result of the actualized intention of the agent be good.

Notice that the term "good" is used in two different ways in this discussion. On the one hand, the "good" is the proper end of the intention of the agent. Janssens has distinguished this inter-pretation of good as mainly psychological, that is, the human actor by nature moves in the direction of what is perceived subjectively as a good. The human person never elect, an end which is perceived as evil. He states, "The reality which is the object of a striving we name a good (in the psychological, not the moral sense of the word)."[96] It is this sense of the term "good" that we used above in the discussion on the *voluntas*.

On the other hand, the "good" is defined as that reality which exists as the "bearer of values" (*draagster van de waarden*). In other words, there is something in the concrete reality *outside* the person that is recognized as embodying desirable qualities. For a number of reasons, one's temporal and spatial condition, for example, the perception of the person may be incomplete or even incorrect.[97] This limitation may result in a lack of correspon-dence between "good" in the first sense (as the end of the agent) and "good" in the second sense (as a reality that embodies value).

The "realized good in all its implications" is a summary of the first and second definitions of "good." The agent must desire good not evil and must attempt to actualize the good desired:

[96] See "Geweten en zedelijke waarde," p. 440.

[97] Cf. "Perspectives and Implications of Some Arguments of Saint Thomas Aquinas," p. 5.

intention (good) $\longleftrightarrow$ consequence (good)
  (embraces   (precipitates
  end and means)   intention and value)

The consequence exists in time as a real entity. It is a "realized good" (objectively good) insofar as its actualized values/disvalues are in proportion. One of these actualized values is the good intention of the agent. It is morally good (subjectively good) insofar as the agent, with good intention, adequate freedom and knowledge, actuates means/end in proportion.

Thus an actualized "good" end exists, not in a vacuum, but in a nexus of reality.[98] It exists as a concrete actualized value only in harmony with its real position. It is not sufficient to intend and to effect *any* congruent pair of means and end. There must be some standard by which one evaluates whether this particular entity as the object of moral activity is good.[99] Or, to put the question in another way, is there not a place for norms and standards of value in Janssens' system? What constitutes the right?

Values

Janssens defines value as that which is worthy of promotion by the human person.[100] "A value is a qualitative relation between a reality which is valuable because of some properties or qualities and a subject able to appreciate that reality ...."[101]

[98] Janssens notes that "*Moral rightness* is a question of truth: an act is morally right when it objectively or in truth is appropriate for realizing our morally good disposition and intention." ("Ontic Good and Evil: Premoral Values and Disvalues," p. 78. Cf. "Perspectives and Implications of Some Arguments of Saint Thomas," pp. 8-9.)

[99] It is this judgment which turns a psychologically "good" intention, the fulfillment of a particular striving, into a morally "good" intention, that which seeks to actuate a premoral value.

[100] Janssens' definitions of the various terms used in these sections can be considered reflective of the contemporary literature on the subject. McCormick has suggested that the 1977 article ("Norms and Priorities in a Love Ethics"), for example, "sums up much of what is being said in recent studies on moral norms" (McCormick, *Notes on Moral Theology: 1965-1980*, p. 693).

[101] "Norms and Priorities in a Love Ethics," p. 210, n. 5. Cf. Paul M. Quay,

> Contact with certain realities evokes a *positive feeling* in us. We experience them in a joyful manner .... In these cases our intentional feelings aim at qualities in these realities that bring us joy .... The objective qualities which our intentional feeling reveals as rejoicing in realities we call values. The concrete reality itself which has these qualities and which is thus valuable, or carries a value, we call *a good.*[102]

Such realities as life, health, pleasure, and joy, as well as cultural values (science, art, etc.) are among those he lists.[103] All values are not yet in existence, but rather the pool of values increases as "new *possibilities* are opened for our activity .... Throughout the course of history we also elaborate new *values.*"[104] Newness does not guarantee that a possibility embodies value. Janssens suggests that time be taken to "work out whether or not something was worthy of man."[105] He, among others, calls the realities which embody premoral values "goods." *Pre*moral indicates that they take on a moral significance only when they are embraced by a human agent in an intentioned act (as indicated above).

"Morality by the Calculation of Values," *Readings in Moral Theology*, 1, pp. 271-272.

[102] "Ontic Good and Evil: Premoral Values and Disvalues," pp. 71-72. In this article Janssens draws on the thinking of Paul Ricoeur (see n. 8, 10) to emphasize the *objective* qualities of the good that embodies value. The positive feelings toward a given object are not the *cause* of the value, they are merely the *response* to something that exists in the external reality.

It is interesting to compare earlier writings. See, for example, "Geweten en zedelijke waarde," pp. 436-437. The ideas expressed in the current work are already a part of Janssens' thinking and moral method ("Geweten en zedelijke waarde" was published in 1966). In the earlier article Janssens draws frankly on the work of Max Scheler, who, no doubt growing out of his roots in Heidegger, had already made a point of emphasizing the feeling component of human striving. Scheler's thinking is important in Janssens' development, as evidenced by rather frequent citations to the German philosopher.

[103] Janssens does not make the precise distinction that others make between physical values and spiritual values. See, for example, Frankena, pp. 47-48. Fuchs makes the point that to qualify as what he terms "human values" such processes as technology and economic advancement must be considered in their interpersonal and social aspects (Joseph Fuchs, "The Absoluteness of Moral Terms," *Readings in Moral Theology*, 1, p. 113).

[104] "Artificial Insemination: Ethical Considerations," p. 10.

[105] Ibid., p. 11.

Material Norms

The call to actualize values is expressed in language as material norms. Such statements are "norms" in that they lay down prescriptive (or proscriptive) statements about actions. They are designated "material" because they describe concrete categories of actions (consequences), that is, actions which realize premoral values. Material norms are those which "grapple with the concreteness of the situation, with its material, in order to assess the various values ...."[106] "In a general way, the concrete, material norms set forth the material content (what is done) of categories of actions and prescribe or forbid these actions as morally right or wrong according as they involve premoral values or disvalues."[107]

The application of these norms in Janssens' method is not absolute. While he suggests that "our first attitude towards concrete, material norms ought to be a willingness to follow them," situations with more than one possibility (a hierarchy of premoral values or disvalues is involved) require an application of the "rules of priority (*ordo caritatis et bonorum*),"[108] to the concrete situation. This statement underscores the teleological focus of Janssens' method. He is resistent to specification of

---

[106] Timothy E. O'Connell, *Principles for a Catholic Morality* (New York: Seabury, 1978) p. 160.

[107] See "Norms and Priorities in a Love Ethics," p. 216. Note that most human activity is not pure, that is to say, actions tend to have mixed results: some premoral values are realized and some premoral disvalues are realized. This is the experience we have of reality. This is precisely the difficulty which Janssens addresses in his distinction between ontic evil and moral evil. See "Ontic Evil and Moral Evil," pp. 133-136; 138-156; and "Ontic Good and Evil: Premoral Values and Disvalues," pp. 80-82.

[108] The "*ordo caritatis*" is for Janssens the primacy of charity as the absolute governing factor in moral action. His Christian personalist method is ordered formally to love of self and neighbor. The absolute value is always the moral goodness of the human person. The "*ordo bonorum*" has to do with ranking values according to how they relate to each other, to the urgency of the matter at hand, to their degree of probable realization, to their long term preservation, and to institutionally protected values. These ideas are treated in greater detail in "Norms and Priorities in a Love Ethics," pp. 219-230.

moral duty in arbitrary reference to pre-standing material norms, but rather prefers to make application to the real situation.

Norms derive principally from the historically gathered wisdom of humanity. Moral science has engaged thinkers throughout history in attempts to put into words the contents of what Janssens calls "affinity knowledge" (*affiniteitskennis*),[109] that is, what human strivings perceive as appropriate realization. As an ever increasing new pool of values presents itself, new values may inform the development of new norms. The real norm of our actions, however, Janssens locates in the concrete, as grasped and approved by what he calls the "moral value notion" (*zedelijk waardebesef*).[110]

Formal Norms

Besides the material norms, derived from the content of human values, we may speak of formal norms. To clarify the distinction between the two we can appeal to Janssens' use of Thomas Aquinas' categories to separate the formal element of the exterior action (the intention, which we treated above) and the material element (the object of the exterior action).[111]

formal component: intention (focused on end)
material component: means (embraced by end)
object (in keeping with reason)[112]

[109] See "Geweten en zedelijke waarde," p. 453. Cf. "Gewetensvorming," p. 455, where Janssens follows approximately the same line of thought.

[110] See "Geweten en zedelijke waarde," p. 453. It is difficult to find a satisfactory English equivalent to this compound Dutch term. Literally the Dutch is *zedelijk*, which means "moral," and *waardebesef*, which has to do with a consciousness, realization, or notion of what is of value. In one sense, it is a subjective appreciation or appropriation of what is a value in the objective world. The Roman Catholic natural law tradition accepts that humankind is capable of seeking after and recognizing the objective good, that which embodies value. Below we will address in some detail Janssens' use of the term.

[111] Note that the means (specifed by the end) are also material constituents of the act. See "Artificial Insemination: Ethical Considerations," p. 15, and "Norms and Priorities in Love Ethics," pp. 207-238, for a thorough discussions of formal and material norms.

[112] See above, pp. 86-87.

While the material norm deals with a concrete reality (embodiment of objective value), the formal norm deals with attitudes or direction.[113] Formal norms generally express in language the ideal of what persons ought to *be* (virtue), rather than to specify actions which embody this ideal. They proclaim: be just, chaste, loving, and so forth. (or they prohibit the negative counterparts [vice]: do not be unjust, promiscuous, hating, etc.). In these examples it is unclear what actions precisely actualize the qualities of the values. Sometimes, however, formal norms are expressed in terms which appear to include a material element. Gula[114] quotes Janssens' explanation of so-called "synthetic" formal norms, which include in their formulation *both* a material and an intentional component. Such activities as stealing, adultery, murder, and so forth, express a concrete action (consequence). They also express a motivational (intentional) and circumstantial component, however, which places them within the realm of formal norms.[115]

Formal norms are those which describe the disposition toward goodness of the person, his/her attitude of love.[116] Janssens offers a specific "personalist criterion:"

> our inner attitude must be such that we are genuinely prepared to place our activity as much as possible at the service of the promotion of the human person (self and others) adequately considered in himself as subject in corporeality and in his openness to the world,

[113] See "Gewetenvorming," pp. 454-455. This is the point which Timothy O'Connell makes so strongly in his article, "The Question of Moral Norms," *AER* 169 (1975) 385. O'Connell argues for the paramount importance of formal norms over material norms, since the former answer a need for direction which has emerged in modern society.

[114] See pp. 56-57.

[115] See "Norms and Priorites in a Love Ethics," p. 216, n. 8. Janssens speaks of such terms as "morally qualifying," that is, they affirm both a premoral disvalue and an immoral execution (actions are done without proportionate reason). In general Janssens seems to emphasize the intentional aspect of formal norms more strongly than others.

[116] These ideas are repeated in many places in the Janssens corpus. See, for example, "Christendom en Geweten," p. 903.

to others, to social groups and to God and to respect the originality of each person in our conduct as much as possible.[117]

It is the primary attitude which must be actualized in all moral activity.[118] Janssens goes so far as to state: "The moral goodness of the person is an absolute value."[119] In this instance the value is expressed not in content (as values embodied in material norms), but in terms of direction. The content of this formal norm can vary.[120] In different concrete situations what preserves and/or promotes the human person is not always the same. *That* the human person is to be promoted does not change.

There is one further point that needs clarification. We can speak of a value as existing, in some way, in both time and place. In a temporal sense, this value stands in time *before* the commission of every human action as its canon of righteous judgment (the objective criterion of the right). It is formal, that is, it expresses an ideal without that ideal being embodied in an act or consequence here and now.[121] What this means cannot be completely predetermined, however. While it is true that certain elements of the human person are given and do not change over time (I am recognizable as myself over the range of my lifetime),

---

[117] "Artificial Insemination: Ethical Considerations," p. 15. This statement summarizes a longer section in which the author explains in detail all the elements of the "personalist criterion" in relation to conciliar document *Gaudium et Spes.* We have looked at the more detailed version in chapter two. Cf. "Personalist Morals," p. 5.

[118] In all his work Janssens expresses a much greater concern for attitudes, the inner dispositions of the moral agent, than he does with actions, which are merely external confirmations of these attitudes. See, for example, "Gewetensvorming," p. 452; "Moderne situatie-ethiek in het licht van de klassieke leer over het geweten," p. 79; "Geweten en zedelijke waarde," p. 452, and "Artificial Insemination: Ethical Considerations," p. 15. It is the attitude of the person that is the dynamic principle that informs his or her moral activity. This is the reason why the formation of conscience is so vital.

[119] "Norms and Priorities in a Love Ethics," p. 229.

[120] Ibid., p. 208.

[121] Janssens allows, however, that we come to an understanding of such values and norms through the experience of history. There are even some thinkers whose work expresses perhaps better than others these insights for the benefit of society. See "Geweten en zedelijke waarde," p. 439.

it is true as well that the human person is an evolving entity. Insight into the nature of slavery or that of women can change the content of the value over time.[122] In this sense "the human person adequately considered" is mediated in the oscillation between that which has been and that which is becoming and is a continually-being-discovered reality. Therefore the normative expression of the value may change.

Secondly, the value may be positioned in space. A deontological approach may locate values arbitrarily outside the person.[123] Janssens, on the other hand, is insistent on the location of value *within* the person. Each man or woman, as an open intentionality, constructs a personal set of values from the common human interaction with the world, others, and God; the content of the set for each person will be unique.[124] Further, as the person freely chooses this experience or that, this actualization over that

[122] We speak here in an existential mode. Certainly one could argue that enslavement of others or oppression of women were and are disvalues apart from the awakening that precipitated the Civil War and the ERA. Yet the incorporation of these insights into the set of human values occurred only at a specific point in the continuum of history. The tree falling unwitnessed in the primal forest, however dead, has no meaning until some adventuresome Dr. Livingston catches the toe of his modern hiking boot in its decaying branches. Therefore the set of values that humankind as a whole or the human person as an individual is required to actualize (or to consider among a pool of possible values/disvalues to be actualized) is limited to those which s/he actually can be responsible to know. Catholic moral tradition has a precedent for this position in her attitude toward impediments to moral responsibility, which may include inculpable ignorance. See, for, example, Timothy E. O'Connell, *Principles for a Catholic Morality*, pp. 47-51.

[123] Or s/he may locate them within but, in a sense, over against the human person. Germain Grisez, *The Way of the Lord Jesus: Christian Moral Principles*, 1 (Chicago: Franciscan Herald, 1983), speaks, for example, of a basic set of human goods which "are aspects of persons, not realities apart from persons" (p. 121) and which flow from an inherent principle to pursue the good (pp. 184-185). Grisez differs from Janssens, however, in that Grisez denies that the human person in him/her self as related to the world, to others, and to God is the ultimate value.

[124] This set is not arbitrary, merely at the whim of the individual. The person is called to be honest in his/her openness toward the real values expressed in his/her relationships. Rather than a subjective set, the set of values is based on objective criteria and ultimately on the prime objective criterion, the human person.

one, s/he reinforces the particular values or attitudes contained in his or her set.

Janssens does not postulate a moral system that excludes all non-subjective criteria for determining morality. First, he offers his formal principle: the promotion in love of the human person adequately considered. This principle serves as an objective criterion to stand before and after the act as the standard of right. This principle exists in time before the person and in space within the person as a motivating attitude. It acts as a rule for evaluation of the good in concrete moral activity. He affirms the importance of material norms which formulate in language that which is objectively of value in actualizing the formal principle. Finally, he stresses the theme of love which motivates all human action. The task remains, however, to join these ideas more clearly to the human agent.

Relating the Components for Moral Evaulation

The subjective and objective components of morality come together in the conscience of each individual person. Janssens' treatment of conscience moves beyond the thinking of Thomas Aquinas (conscience as the judgment of practical reason) to define a much richer phenomenon.[125] Janssens terms conscience "the awareness of our moral striving both as a disinterested and unconditional consciousness of moral value and as an absolute and unconditional aiming toward morally valuable actions."[126]

The latter aspect, a dynamic orientation to the moral good (we shall designate this aspect as conscience/1), [127] is endemic to the human person as human.[128] At this level the human person

[125] "*Synderesis et Conscientia*: Student Notes for the Course in History of Moral Theology," Louvain: American College, 1975 (Mimeographed), p. 62. Much of Janssens work, perhaps more so earlier material, assumes this notion of conscience. In "Ontic Evil and Moral Evil," for example, Janssens spends a great deal of time exposing Thomas' thinking on the matter.

[126] "Geweten en zedelijke waarde," p. 455.

[127] A parallel model to Janssens' exposition of conscience is that offered by O'Connell, *Principles for a Catholic Morality*, chapter 8. While O'Connell's three levels of conscience (see pp. 89-92) do not express precisely what Janssens does,

is always responsible for the love that he bears to truth and to the good, and every act which embodies this love increases his moral perfection. ... it is the love of moral good which animates what he does, and it is precisely the maintaining of this love which promotes his moral perfection.[129]

This striving attitude toward what is morally good becomes stronger and stronger within the person as s/he exercises faithfulness to and involvement in the capacity. The more I love justice and the more I exercise justice, the more justice becomes a part of my natural affinity and action (virtue).[130]

Justice, or any other virtue, does not exist in itself, but only as it is embodied in certain concrete realities. This brings us to the second aspect of conscience. Every person has a certain "content" by which she evaluates what is the good—a pool of models, values, norms, and so forth, against which to judge the moral possibilities of this or that concrete act. Janssens speaks of a "moral value notion"[131] which abides within the person and perceives moral value in a disinterested and unconditional manner[132] (conscience/2). This pool is formed through the process of selective openness to the reality offered to the person. I cannot apprehend all possible values. Either because of my limitations or the historical limits—not all possibilities are yet available. In addition, my free choice selects some values and discards others,

they are helpful, I think, in understanding Janssens' approach. Here I borrow O'Connell's designations and apply them for clarity to Janssens' work.

[128] Janssens distinguishes between individual strivings, which spontaneously seek their own proper end (hunger seeks food, for example) in things outside the person, and the integrating moral striving, which sees beyond the specified inclinations to what is morally apt in the actions of the person. See "Geweten en zedelijke waarde," pp. 443-444.

[129] *Freedom of Conscience and Religious Freedom*, p. 81. There is an interesting side note here. In the footnote appended to this section (see n. 22, p. 115), Janssens notes that his argument to support religious freedom (the point of this particular book) rests on the personalist criterion, that is, the inviolability of the individual's perspective. He further notes the connection between this dignity of the human person and the Catholic moral "principle of subsidiarity."

[130] See "Geweten en zedelijke waarde (II)," p. 33.

[131] See "Geweten en zedelijke waarde," p. 442.

[132] "Geweten en zedelijke waarde," p. 445.

presumably because they do not fit my image of who I am or whom I choose to become. [133]

Each person is responsible for the objective content of his/her moral value notion, which has been formed through honest interaction with the world. Further more, each person is responsible to continue to respond to the objective reality outside the self as a check on the adequacy of his or her own set. [134] Following Newman, and in keeping with his own Christian personalism, Janssens notes that this interaction with reality is implicitly a religious experience, that is, an experience of God as the source of our absolute obligation. [135] In addition, part of the external content which is available for experience is Christian revelation and tradition.

The third aspect of conscience has to do with concrete judgment in a particular situation (conscience/3). This judgment is impowered by the dynamic striving toward good (conscience/1) and informed by the ever-in-dialogue-with-reality content of the moral value notion (conscience/2). Whether or not this specific action embodies a moral value is the practical judgment of the conscience. Ultimately, morality is judged by the subject on the basis of the motivation and choice embodied in the object of each act, but with the objective check provided by the informed and open moral value notion. While the person may choose to ignore the truth of the objective data, or may choose to remain uninfor-

[133] We must underline again that this process is neither totally subjective nor arbitrary for Janssens, but is based on objective criteria.

[134] Janssens perceives this desire to learn more and more about concrete reality as a natural drive, so that humanity always seeks the complete truth, "toward the unveiling of all reality." See "Geweten en zedelijke waarde," pp. 447-448.

[135] In much of his writing Janssens does not clarify or distinguish the unthematized experience of God that is common to all persons and the thematized experience that is available in Christian tradition. A strong presentation of explicitly Christian input can be found in "Christendom en Geweten," pp. 901-904; *Freedom of Conscience and Religious Freedom*, pp. 86-90; "Humanisme en personalisme," *Dietsche Warande en Belfort* 107 (1962) pp. 718-724. See also a more concise but comparable treatment in "Artificial Insemination: Ethical Considerations," p. 15.

med as to what available objective data there are, he or she is still responsible for that data in every concrete moral evaluation.[136] To be judged praiseworthy or blameworthy a person's actions are accountable to objective criteria.

We must not forget that Janssens' prime objective norm is the human person considered in relationship. This criterion is not a constant, however. Conscience/1 and conscience/2 partially define the "already me"—the person I am by nature and s/he whom I have become in the selective appropriation of values, and so forth, from my relationships. There is another aspect of the "already me," however. Conscience/3, the judgment factor in any categorical moral decision making situation, has its part to play. In accordance with my general tendency toward the good and appealing for congruence with my internal set of values, and so forth, I judge the moral appropriateness of this act. A choice in accord with conscience /1 and /2 begets a single real act that has a consequence beyond me and a consequence within me, namely, adding to or creating the already me indicated above. With each act I remain old yet I become new. At each act, the human person, the final criterion in Janssens' method for morality, becomes something slightly different.

This, however, is not the complete picture. We must raise the discussion of such activity to the macro level and look at it from the point of view of all human persons engaged in the same self-creating activity.[137] All seek the good (conscience/1). There is a

---

[136] Janssens is optimistic in his assertion that one's conscience will stand as an objective witness to the presence of good or evil action. See "Geweten en zedelijk waarde," p. 442.

[137] This is necessary since the human person adequately considered is not meant to mean simply this individual person—that would eliminate all but pure subjectivity—but rather the human person in general, as humanity is perceived at this point on the continuum of time. As humanity grows in its understanding of itself, it is always something new. Humanity to the ancient Hebrew people did not include women on a level with man (as witnessed by the Ten Commandments, which place coveted wives on the level with cattle); humanity in early America did not include blacks within its definition. Today we have a fuller definition of humanity, which must inform the norm presented by Janssens in a richer way. It is possible to assume that future knowledge will further enrich the norm's content.

pool of values, and so forth, which inform the human community *qua* human community at any point in time (conscience/2). The human community chooses to self-create (conscience/3) in congruence with its own collective subjective striving and moral value notion, its understanding of what it means to be human.

This broader cultural pool informs the individual pool (individual moral value notion) and acts as a check upon it. As the human community advances along the continuum of time toward its own definition and actualization in historic reality, what it means to be human *now* acts as the value pool and check on whether newness is equatable with good. Here, in the present moment, is the place where the individual act of the person intersects with the objective norm. What is existentially right (objective truth as now known) is that which conforms to the good as it has been thematized thus far.

In short, the human conscience is the medium through which the subjective human act confronts objective moral criteria in order to evaluate what is (subjectively) good against what is the (objectively) right. In a teleological system, such as that proposed by Louis Janssens, predisposing criteria such as values and the norms they inform must await evaluation in their embodiment in the total act of the person.

In his frankly Christian and frankly teleological moral method Janssens affirms: 1) there is a growing objective reality which is available to the human person in moral decision making, 2) the will of God is expressed in this objective reality to be discovered gradually and always in an incomplete manner, 3) the subject is responsible to this objective content insofar as s/he has apprehended it, 4) the morality of actions is finally determined by the criterion of the person in the completeness of the moral act.

CHAPTER FOUR

INTERFACE WITH ROMAN CATHOLIC MORAL METHOD

The Methodology of Vatican II

The Second Vatican Council set out initially to produce a separate and thoroughgoing document on morality. A schema, *De ordine morali*, had been prepared for the bishops gathered for the 1962 opening session. It sought, according to Philippe Delhaye, "to restore the repressive aspect of the teaching of Pius XII."[1] It proposed to denounce "subjectivism and situationalism" as well as to emphasize "the objective and absolute nature of the moral order." It went on record as suspicious of a moral theology grounded in charity, since such a starting point carried the danger of "sentimentalism and an abandonment of moral precepts."

The spirit blew in other directions, however. Along with the rest of the predictable pre-conciliar schemata, *De ordine morali*, was rejected. When the enthusiastic assembly, composed mostly of *periti* from fields other than moral theology, set out anew to formulate what would become the official documents of Vatican II, no text specifically addressed to moral theology was produced.

An innovative personalist ground for moral theology can, however, be detected in the text of *Gaudium et Spes*.[2] Its seeds

[1] Philippe Delhaye, "The Contribution of Vatican II to Moral Theology," *Concilium* 75 (1972) 58-59.

[2] As we proceed with a brief summary of the personalism evident in this document, we shall refer by footnote to parallel texts in Janssens' work, adding the year of publication. Rereading *Gaudium et Spes* after several months of work on Janssens' material, I am struck with the remarkable congruence between the two. This congruence has been emphasized by Janssens himself in such articles as "Artifical Insemination: Ethical Considerations," especially pp. 4-14. The footnotes provided will allow the reader to draw his/her own conclusions.

were already planted and growing in the contemporary European atmosphere.[3] Its text, published on December 7, 1965, took its keynote from the conciliar renewal in scripture and reaffirmed as its ground.[4] the charity of Christ, which permeated the council in its attitudes and in its documents. Its pages exhibit an "evident openness to fundamental elements in the intellectual climate of 20th-century civilization, to the dimensions of human culture opened up by advances in the historical, social, and psychological sciences," according to one commentator.[5] Further, even when the document seems merely to repeat the teachings of earlier twentieth century popes, "the very restatement of well-known passages sometimes uncovers a nuance of personalism that owes much to later Catholic thought in France and elsewhere."[6] *Gaudium et Spes*, with its focus on the human person existing in a modern historical context, is a watershed document, heralding a new direction for Roman Catholic moral theology in the latter half of the twentieth century.

The document begins by locating the human person in self and in his/her relationships. It seeks to discover "the meaning of his individual and collective strivings,"[7] and "the destiny of reality and of humanity."[8] The second major section treats what it terms "problems of special urgency," namely the family, cultural, socio-economic, and political life. The inviolable dignity of humanity deserves to be supported by the political, social, and economic order, because "the benefits of culture ought to be and actually can be extended to everyone."[9]

---

[3] Noonan suggests that the phenomenological thinking and existential ferment that characterized earlier twentieth century Europe "became fecund influences on Catholic thought." See John T. Noonan, Jr., *Contraception* (New York: New American Library, 1967) p. 573.

[4] See Delhaye, pp. 60 ff., for a discussion of these ideas.

[5] Donald R. Campion, "The Church Today," in Abbott, p. 185. The translation of the texts of Vatican II used throughout this section is that of Walter M. Abbott, general editor, *The Documents of Vatican II* (New York: America, 1966).

[6] Campion, p. 185.

[7] Cf. "Geweten en zedelijke waarde" (1966) p. 455.

[8] *Gaudium et Spes*, 3.

[9] *Gaudium et Spes*, 9. Cf. *Droits personnels et autorité* (1954) p. 17.

A closer look at the text reveals the frankly personalist thrust. Part I, chapter one, characterizes the human person as imaged in God[10] who is his/ her destiny[11]. S/he is body and soul, one entity which shares identity with material creation[12] and at the same time moves beyond the material to seek more and more the content of truth, under the guidance of the Holy Spirit.[13] The person is free[14] and responsible for his/her actions.[15] The conscience, which abides at the depth of the human person, offers

> a law which he does not impose on himself, but which holds him to obedience. Always summoning him to love good and avoid evil, the voice of conscience can when necessary speak to his heart more specially: do this, shun that. For man has in his heart a law written by God. To obey it is the very dignity of man; according to it he will be judged.[16]

In free actions, the human person seeks goodness[17] expressed precisely in love of God and love of neighbor.[18] This "brotherly charity"[19] is the revelatory sign of God's presence.[20]

Humanity is perceived as limited yet called to perfection in a "higher life."[21] "Pulled by manifold attractions, he is constantly forced to choose among them and to renounce some."[22] S/he is

[10] *Gaudium et Spes*, 12, 18. Cf. *Personalisme en democratisering* (1957) p. 29.

[11] *Gaudium et Spes*, 14. Cf. *Personne et société* (1939) pp. 213-215; 238-243; and *Personalisme en democratisering*, pp. 22-28.

[12] *Gaudium et Spes*, 14. Cf. *Personne et société*, pp. 199-206; and *Personalisme en democratisering*, pp. 32-34.

[13] *Gaudium et Spes*, 15. Cf. *Personalisme en democratisering*, p. 22.

[14] *Gaudium et Spes*, 17. Cf. *Personne et société*, 211.

[15] *Gaudium et Spes*, 31. It is impossible to miss the reprised themes of Janssens' personalist thinking in this document. The catalogue of the characteristics of the human person are nearly identical to those of the Flemish theologian. See chapter two, above.

[16] *Gaudium et Spes*, 16. Cf. *Personalisme en democratisering*, p. 30.

[17] *Gaudium et Spes*, 17.

[18] *Gaudium et Spes*, 16.

[19] Janssens, as we have noted many times above, speaks of the treatment of the *evenaaste*.

[20] *Gaudium et Spes*, 21.

[21] *Gaudium et Spes*, 10.

[22] *Gaudium et Spes*, 10. These ideas are congruent with Janssens' thinking. As we noted earlier, his concept of ontic evil, developed in detail after the council in

an "unsolved puzzle" to which God alone holds the solution.[23] God is both the root and terminus of human dignity.[24]

Part I, chapter two, underlines the communal nature of humanity and the interdependence of persons and society.

> Man's social nature makes it evident that the progress of the human person and the advance of society itself hinge on each other.[25] For the beginning, the subject and the goal of all social institutions is and must be the human person,[26] which for its part and by its very nature stands completely in need of social life.[27] This social life is not something added on to man.[28] Hence, through his dealings with others, through reciprocal duties, and through fraternal dialogue he develops all his gifts and is able to rise to his destiny.[29]

The document stresses the promotion of the common good to serve the human person, whose rights and duties are inviolable.[30] The human person is characterized as the foundational value, to be reverenced as "another self,"[31] unique and equal in dignity to every other person.[32] Persons and associations must "cultivate in themselves the moral and social virtues, and promote them in society."[33] Resources are to be used to bring a higher degree of culture to all humanity.[34] "The norm of human activity is this:

1972, was already established in a very early article, "Tijd en ruimte in de moraal" (1947) pp. 181-197.

[23] *Gaudium et Spes*, 21.

[24] *Gaudium et Spes*, 21.

[25] Cf. *Personalisme en democratisering*, p. 33; *Personne et société*, pp. 294-295; 301-302.

[26] Cf. *Droits personnels et autorité* (1954) p. 17.

[27] See Janssens' early work, "Liefde en sociaal leven" (1951), especially pp. 21-27, which details human need for social life in all its forms.

[28] Cf. *Personalisme en democratisering*, p. 57; *Droits personnels et autorité*, p. 18 ("notre sociabilité n'est pas quelque chose d'accessoire").

[29] *Gaudium et Spes*, 25.

[30] *Gaudium et Spes*, 26. Cf. "Rechten van de mens" (1952) p. 526.

[31] *Gaudium et Spes*, 27. Cf. *Personalisme en democratisering*, p. 35; "Liefde en sociaal leven," p. 8. This is, of course, one of Janssens' major themes.

[32] *Gaudium et Spes*, 29.

[33] *Gaudium et Spes*, 30.

[34] *Gaudium et Spes*, 31. Again we are confronted with a recurrent Janssenist theme. See "De rechten van de mens," p. 525; *Droits personnels et autorité*, pp. 5-9; and *Personalisme en democratisering*, pp. 32-34, for example.

that in accord with the divine plan and will, it should harmonize with the genuine good of the human race, and allow men as individuals and as members of society to pursue their total vocation and fulfill it."[35]

This personalist foundation is applied in Part Two of the document. One can detect the beginnings of a moral method at work, indeed of a personalist moral method which, at the very least, is consistent with that of Louis Janssens:

> ... the moral aspect of any procedure does not depend solely on sincere intentions or on an evaluation of motives. It must be determined by objective standards. These, based on the nature of the human person and his acts, preserve the full sense of mutual self-giving and human procreation in the context of true love.[36]

By now it is patent that the moral methodology of Louis Janssens compares not only favorably but almost exactly to that of the conciliar document, *Gaudium et Spes*. Both are based in the personalist understanding of the human person. Both focus on the evolving objective criterion of the good of the human person, rather than on predetermined arbitrary rules.

We could illustrate these themes further by an analysis of *Dignitatis Humanae Personae*,[37] whose themes are congruent to those of *Gaudium et Spes* or to *Lumen Gentium*, with its emphasis on a new dialogical model of the church, the people of God,[38]

---

[35] *Gaudium et Spes*, 35.

[36] *Gaudium et Spes*, 51. This citation, of course, indicates an application to a particular moral problem taken up in this practical second section, that of conception regulation. We shall explore Janssens' approach to this topic later. It is important not to miss the point made here, however. While the context is specific application, the principle applied does not appear to be one limited to *this* application. Rather, it would seem that the document is indicating a more general principle: the objective standard of human moral action is the nature of the human person and his/her acts. (Cf. 57, 63, 73, 77, which apply the principle to the other "problems of special urgency." In each case, the criterion for morality is the teleological assessment: what preserves and advances the dignity of the human person?) As seen earlier in the text, the nature of the human person is a conscious, free, responsible material being who exists in relationship and who finds completion in the divine.

[37] See 1 and 2, for example.

[38] *Lumen Gentium*, 9-17.

and the vested place of the laity.[39] At any rate it is apparent that the Second Vatican Council, while it did not set out to produce a "new" moral methodology, did provide the ground for a shift from the legalism and ecclesial positivism of the earlier twentieth century to a personalistic system of teleology.

The Natural Law Tradition

If we are to see how Janssens' thinking intersects with that of traditional Catholic moral method, an understanding of the common uses of the term natural law is necessary.

Definition and Distinctions

Natural Law as a Basis for Moral Knowledge (Metaethical Level)

The history of moral theology chronicles a variety of definitions of the term "natural law." This largesse often is the cause of misunderstanding. We shall try to correct this difficulty. The most fundamental premise of the natural law, at the metaethical level,[40] provides a means of verifying moral judgments and

[39] *Lumen Gentium*, 35 and 37, for example.

[40] Metaethics is concerned with the epistemological question: how do we validate the "ought" statements that we make? See Robert M. Veatch, "Does Ethics Have an Empirical Basis?" *Hastings Center Report* 1 (1973) 51. Veatch explores the various theories of metaethics and opts for empirical metaethical absolutism, that is, the premise that human beings are capable of identifying what in reality is good, or, to use Janssens' term, embodies value. Cf. J. J. C. Smart, *Ethics, Persuasion and Truth* (Boston: Routledge and Kegan Paul, 1984) p. 7. See David F. Kelly, "Schema for Ethical Questions and Answers," (Mimeographed), p. 3, which follows Veatch's categories. Kelly includes in his definition the Christian theological presupposition that there is a God involved in creation. In other work Kelly provides a handy chart for sorting out the pertinent systems. See *The Emergence of Roman Catholic Medical Ethics in North America*, p. 452. Cf. Fuchs, pp. 6-7, especially; and Frankena, pp. 80-85. If humanity does not have an ability to know the good and likewise a faculty to seek and to actuate that good, once perceived, moral science is meaningless.

systems. The first principle is that humanity has a natural capacity to know the good, a "moral sense" which is inherent, or "natural" to being-as-human.[41] Because I am human, I "see" that ... an event is morally reprehensible at this time or is morally necessary in order to satisfy the requirements of freedom, utility, and so forth, or perhaps is morally permissible as a procedure which need not be morally forbidden but is not required either."[42] At the metaethical level, then, "natural law" merely makes a descriptive statement about what it means to be human. The empirical judgment made is that human beings have the capacity to know what is moral. It is not a statement about biology; it is a statement of what is unique and proper to humanity.[43] If this statement is accepted, it becomes the "law" which frames and judges human action at the normative level. Who I am (ontology, asserted at the metaethical level [empirical metaethical absolutism]) then becomes the standard (morality, at the normative level) of what I do to create myself.

Further, the human person has the capacity and the tendency to seek the good as end of his/her actions.[44] This perspective is consistent with Catholicism's optimistic view of creation. As Keane notes:

This metaethical premise does not demand a Christian or even a theistic stance. As Schüller observes, "So far as I know, no traditional Catholic theologian or philosopher has ever doubted that men and women, whether they believe in God or not, are able to make objectively valid value judgments." See *Wholly Human: Essays on the Theory and Language of Morality* (Washington: Georgetown University, 1986) p. 52.

[41] Kelly, p. 245, n. 4. This is Janssens' assertion as well. See above p. 53.

[42] Veatch, p. 63.

[43] On natural law theory, see Josef Fuchs, *Natural Law: A Theological Investigation* (New York: Sheed and Ward, 1965); O'Connell, pp. 134-143; Gula, pp. 34-53; Curran, *Directions*, pp. 119-172; Philip S. Keane, *Sexual Morality: A Catholic Perspective* (New York: Paulist, 1977) pp. 43-46. Eric D'Arcy offers a thorough discussion on the topic in his article, "Natural Law," *Encyclopedia of Bioethics*, pp. 1131-1137. Further insight and an appreciation of the variety of approaches to natural law as well as a taste of the rich fare produced in recent years can be found generously referenced in McCormick, *Notes on Moral Theology: 1965-1980*, pp. 13-29; p. 575, n. 4; pp. 696-697, n. 31.

[44] Cf. p. 53.

> Probably the single most · significant element in the traditional
> Roman Catholic understanding of morality is natural law ....
> Roman Catholicism has just reason to be proud of the natural law
> tradition.[45] The Catholic belief in the basic goodness of human
> persons and human communities is rooted in the natural law
> tradition.[46]

Imbedded in this affirmation are two conclusions about human nature. The first is that there is no conflict between nature and grace.[47] Or, to put it another way, no person escapes the offer of relationship with God. Therefore we can affirm with Rahner that human nature is good, bathed as it is in God's favor.[48] This assumption is apparent in *Gaudium et Spes*, as we saw above, and has been documented in our lengthy exposition of Janssens' personalism in chapter two. There is a strong connection between Janssens' (and others') trust in the veracity of conscience and an acceptance of natural law theory. A presupposition that human nature is essentially oriented to the good supports the affirmation that conscience is a valid norm for moral decison making.

This leads to a second conclusion. Revelation adds no new content to the natural law. Whether or not there is a unique Christian ethic has been the subject of intense debate in recent years.[49] McCormick has surveyed the literature on the subject. He suggests that Schüller, for one, interprets natural law as a *predisposition* to revelation.[50] Says McCormick: "The fact that

[45] Curran makes the same point. See *Directions*, p. 120.

[46] Keane, *Sexual Morality*, pp. 43-44.

[47] This position is frankly Roman Catholic. Protestant theology, especially Lutheran, tends to maintain a dichotomy between unredeemed, sinful human nature and graced faith, the gift of God. See discussion in D'Arcy, pp. 1133-1134.

[48] Rahner refers to the "supernatural existential." See *Foundations of Christian Faith*, pp. 126-127. Cf. "Justified and Sinner at the Same Time," in *Theological Investigations*, 6 (1974), pp. 221-223. While we cannot deny the existence of original sin as a limiting factor in the exercise of this goodness, this limitation seems less central when viewed over against the reality of the gift of grace. This view is in harmony with Janssens' perennially optimistic approach to humankind.

[49] We have already cited MacNamara's comprehensive treatment of the topic (*Faith and Ethics*) above.

[50] Cf. the recently translated collection of Schüller's essays, which deal with the same topic, Bruno Schüller, *Wholly Human: Essays on the Theory and Language of Morality* (Washington: Georgetown University, 1986).

natural morality concerns [human beings] is for man his obe-
diential potency that the law of Christ can concern him." [51]
Therefore revelation is perceived as adding a thematization of
what is already present in all humanity as potency, or unthematized direction. [52] This idea seems congruent with Janssens' position. [53] Revelation serves to articulate formal norms as motivation for action. Those material norms which are contained in the
scriptural text seem only to articulate or to specify what is
already present or available within general human experience. [54]
These constitute the "religious extra" of revelation, which flows
from (since God's expression in different arenas is not in conflict
with itself), but is not identical with, the natural law.

Natural Law as a Set of Principles (Normative Level)

At the normative level natural law may be taken to mean a set
of principles for action. Pre-Vatican II Catholic theology often

---

[51] McCormick, *Notes on Moral Theology: 1965-1980*, p. 129. McCormick's
analysis includes comments on Bruno Schüller's German article "Zur theo-
logischen Diskussion über die lex naturalis," *Theologie und Philosophie* 41 (1966)
481-503. It is Schüller's opinion that he elaborates here.

[52] Häring takes a similar approach. He agrees that the genesis of natural law
may have been a spontaneous understanding of the relationship to one's fellow
men—without knowing the radical implication that all men could really be "fellow
men".... But ... there is a great difference between a human experience which
practically or implicitly includes such a principle and an actual capacity to
conceptualize such an experience.

Häring sees revelation as adding an awareness and understanding which would
be impossible either because of the limits of human intelligence or by temporal
limitations. See Bernard Häring, "Dynamism and Continuity in a Personalistic
Approach to Natural Law," Gene H. Outka and Paul Ramsey, eds., *Norm and
Context in Christian Ethics* (New York: Charles Scribner's, 1968) pp. 202, 204.

[53] Part of this thematization for Janssens is the scriptural articulation of what
he terms "the ultimate sense of moral actions." See "Christus en de moraal,"
Christendon en secularisatie (Antwerpse Theologische Studieweek, 1969), Ant-
werpen: Patmos, 1970, p. 74.

[54] "Christ is Gospel not Law. Christ is not Law, but Fulfillment of the Law,"
affirms Schüller. *Wholly Human: Essays on the Theory and Language of Morality*,
p. 26.

has emphasized only one aspect of this level.[55] Accepting the first principle noted above,[56] it posits, in addition, a set of values or principles which exist in "nature" and which are, at least to some extent, restricted to biological aspects of the human person.[57] Other aspects—psychological, social, spiritual, contextual, for example—tend to be ignored. This set of principles has its grounding in a presupposition that the divinely initiated world is basically unchangeable; therefore it is possible to derive constant objective moral norms.[58] Reason not only is able to discover these norms but must respect them in choosing options for moral action.

The first, and considered to be universal, principle of natural law at the normative level is devoid of specified content (the known good must be done and the good must be loved).[59] It merely articulates the normative conclusion of the statement made above that human beings are capable of knowing and seeking the good. If being-as-human (human "nature") is oriented to the good, it follows logically that one ought actuate one's teleology in that good.

[55] Personalism represents another approach to the normative level of natural law.

[56] See, for example, Grisez's treatment in *Contraception and the Natural Law* (Milwaukee: Bruce, 1964) p. 62.

[57] Grisez locates these principles within the human person. He contends that "this general norm of practical reason and the other basic prescriptions ... are not in any sense imperatives from without. They [rather] express the necessities which reason must determine for itself if intelligent action is to be possible." See p. 62.

[58] The difference between the revisionist (Janssens *et al.*) position and this one is the presumption here of the absolute nature of such principles *as they are able to be discovered with certitude* in what Vacek calls "an intricately interrelated and evolving world." (See Edward V. Vacek, "Proportionalism: One View of the Debate," *TS* 46 [1985] 294.) The revisionists do not deny, necessarily, that such principles may indeed exist. Vacek goes on to note, however, that "an absolute' would have to be formulated in such a way as to ensure in advance that ... the involvement of God in the world [and other factors of variety] will never introduce any significant differences. This seems impossible if one takes historicity seriously."

[59] This is Häring's formulation of the fundamental precept of the natural law as understood in Catholic moral theology. See Bernard Häring, *The Law of Christ*, 1: *General Moral Theology* (Westminster: Newman, 1961) p. 245.

There is a tendency to expand this conclusion, however, and to see in human biology a reliable template for morality. This application of natural law (natural law physicalism) is a kind of biological determinism which the moral agent is expected to respect in decision making. It functions at the normative level, reducing created human nature to its physical and biological aspects. In this interpretation of natural law, it is biological laws which appear to enjoy divine approval, since God is the author and architect of biological, physical creation. [60] As Gula puts it, "Stated boldly, physicalism understands nature [Gula refers to biology] as the viceroy of God. The rule of God and the rule of nature are practically one. In nature, God speaks. The structures and actions of nature are the expressions of God's actions on humankind." [61] The human person must seek the principles within his/her biology and must follow them. [62]

The standard of moral judgment ("conformity with nature") is the fixed (biological) nature of the human being; the process of moral judgment here ("follow reason") is simply a check on the congruence between a static reality and the specific action under evaluation. The content of the good can be defined definitively in advance of the action by objective norms which must be obeyed. Moral behavior is conformity to norm (deontology) without consideration of consequences or motive; immoral behavior is "intrinsic evil." [63] In this approach to natural law the human

[60] John J. Reed concludes that it is "law" precisely because it is the order established by God. See "Natural Law, Theology and the Church," *TS* 26 (1965) 40-64.

[61] Gula, p. 35.

[62] Grisez concludes to a set of principles for human action based on what he calls the "basic tendencies" which "prefigure everything man can achieve" (see p. 64). Such tendencies include procreation, since "Few normal people fail to marry and few married couples who are not sterile fail to have children" (see p. 78).

[63] This term is perfectly consistent when one eliminates elements other than norm (e.g. consequences, motive, circumstances) and postulates the possibility of absolute clarity in knowledge of God's will. We shall call this approach to defining morality the act-object approach. We shall treat the distinction between it and Janssens's intention-end approach (see chapter three above) in the following section.

person is subordinated to other considerations rather than seen as a value in him/herself.

This second approach to natural law affords a basis for conclusions in bioethics,[64] and supports the current condemnation by the ecclesial magisterium of what has been termed a "morally forbidden category of sexual practices."[65] The emphasis is on "the givenness of biological imperatives," as Noonan notes.[66] Therefore a presumed biological teleology[67] becomes the criterion for moral judgments.[68] There are two subtle implications in this interpretation of the natural law. A first implication is: although there is a human process at work in discovering what God has placed in nature, there is no real novelty, since God acts outside of and before time. The following statement from the Vatican's 1976 "Declaration on Certain Questions Concerning Sexual Ethics" illustrates this statement:

> Therefore there can be no true promotion of man's dignity unless the essential order of his nature is respected. Of course, in the history of civilization many of the concrete conditions and needs of human life have changed and will continue to change. But all evolution of morals and every type of life must be kept within the limits imposed by the immutable principles based upon every human person's constitutive elements and essential relations—elements and relations which transcend historical contingency.[69]

[64] See D'Arcy, p. 1130. Cf. Keane, p. 45; Kelly, pp. 244-245; Curran, *Directions*, pp. 126-127; and Gula, p. 35, for example.

[65] Bruce Williams, "Homosexuality: the New Vatican Statement," *TS* 48 (1987) 267.

[66] Noonan, p. 573.

[67] This biological teleology is not incompatible with what we have called deontology above. In a closed or "classic world view" system there is no conflict between the pre-given (deontological) norms and the end (*telos*). As Gula notes, p. 18, "the classicist worldview works on the assumption that the world is a finished product.... A good look grasps immutable essences which yield a high degree of certitude and can be stored up to remain valid forever." (Cf. Curran, *Directions*, pp. 138-139.) Gula's "good look" ought to determine the meaning and destination of creatures, which data can then be formulated in norms. Morality becomes a congruence between the norms (formulated deontologically) and the action (which moves—if moral—toward its proper end).

[68] A rather amusing account of application to the act of human sexual intercourse can be enjoyed in Noonan, pp. 289-291.

The existential component is reduced to discovery, although it appears that some aspects are already clear. Clear to *whom* brings us to the second implication: there is a special competence or "inside track" to God's design that is assigned to the church as institution.[70] Again from the Roman document on sexual ethics:

> Furthermore, Christ instituted his Church as "the pillar and bulwark of truth" [cites I Tim.]. With the Holy Spirit's assistance, she ceaselessly preserves and transmits without error the truths of the moral order, and she authentically interprets not only the revealed positive law but "also ... those principles of the moral order which have their origin in human nature itself" [cites *Dignitatis Humanae* and other sources] and which concern man's full development and sanctification.[71]

A more recent document reiterates the same basic presumption:

> [the Catholic moral perspective] finds support in the more secure findings of the natural sciences [in the complex issue of homosexuality], which have their own legitimate and proper methodology and field of inquiry.
>
> However, the Catholic moral viewpoint is founded on human reason illumined by faith and is consciously motivated by the desire to do the will of God, our Father. The church is thus in a position to learn from scientific discovery *but also to transcend the horizons of science and to be confident that her more global vision does greater justice to the rich reality of the human person* [my emphasis]....[72]

It is in this "more global vision" that the document condemns homosexuality as "a more or less strong tendency ordered toward an intrinsic moral evil ...." Both documents assume a biological determination (a law within nature)[73] and a special ecclesial

---

[69] Cf. Anthony Kosnik *et al.*, eds., *Human Sexuality: New Directions in American Catholic Thought* (New York: Paulist, 1977), Appendix 3, pp. 300-301.

[70] Here we witness the coming together of the metaethical level of ecclesiastical positivism (see Kelly, p. 452) with physicalism.

[71] Kosnick, p. 301.

[72] "The Pastoral Care of Homosexual Persons," *Origins* 16 (1986) 378-379.

[73] The "bottom line" for the document's condemnation of certain practices and tendencies is the conclusion that "homosexual acts, however noble their conscious inspiration might sometimes be, are inauthentic expressions of sexual love insofar as they lack the sexual complementarity and potential fruitfulness demanded by the nuptial truth of created persons embodied as male and female."

competence to understand and to teach. Both documents urge conformity to and respect for the "natural" finality of certain processes (act-object morality).

Discussion

Where does Janssens fit in all of this? His starting point is theological. God is the fulcrum of creation and of human activity. The natural law is, in terminology familiar in Roman Catholic moral tradition, participation in the being of God. First, God is present in the nature and activity of the human being[74]. The power and activity of human reason are the manifestation of the divine image, that which sets persons apart from other entities in the created world. "As image of God, man is the autonomous subject of his own actions; as rational creature, he is an active participant in divine providence, to the extent that he directs his own actions and dominates other creatures."[75] Janssens locates the responsibility for moral activity strongly within the subject. The human person is not merely an observer of existential reality, s/he is a responsible co-creator of what is and what will be.

Secondly, God is present and knowable in creation. It is here that the human being, as a fundamental openness, discovers

See Bruce Williams, "Homosexuality: The New Vatican Statement," *TS* 48 (1987) 262. While Williams' treatment is restrained to the point of affirmation of the document (noting, for example, its use of scripture as basing the heterosexual spousal relationship as normative [see pp. 260-261]), it cannot deny its physicalist conclusions (homosexual acts "lack an essential and indispensable finality" [see p. 261]).

[74] In his earlier work, of which this is an example, Janssens tends to use the term "human *nature*." Later, his terminology becomes more nuanced as he speaks more about the "human *person*" as the elemental criterion for morality. Cf., for example, "Moderne situatie-ethiek in het licht van de klassieke leer over het geweten," p. 74, where he cites human nature [*menselijke natuur*] as the general valid objective norm of morality; with later works, such as "Artificial Insemination: Ethical Considerations," p. 13, where the stress is on the human person adequately considered.

[75] "Considerations on *Humanae Vitae*," p. 238. Janssens is summarizing his reading of Thomas Aquinas, *Summa Theologica*, I,II, prologue; *Summa contra Gentiles*, bk. III, c. 113; *Summa Theologica*, I, II, q. 91, art. 2.

God's will, the "final norm of morality." [76] It is this second point that serves as a corrective to the apparent subjectivism that results from placing responsibility on the person for decision making. Janssens makes a distinction that is imperative for clarifying his position, particularly in juxtaposition to the second approach to natural law described above. He begins with the question: how can creation demonstrate what God wants? Initially he reflects on this question from the vantage point of Thomas Aquinas:

> As far as the generic natural law goes, this problem did not strike him [Thomas] as too complicated. He said, in effect, that the divine intentions are reflected and expressed so clearly in the biological reality of men and animals that it suffices to study them to discern immediately (*absolute apprehendere*) the finality determined by God in the order of nature. [77]

For Janssens, however, the question is more complicated than it was for the angelic doctor, whose world view was static. "Our affirmations [regarding the clear finality of "nature"] have become more prudent," states Janssens. [78] Modern anthropology and the natural sciences have made us suspicious of the clarity and certainty of human knowledge. We see it in a more historical perspective, that is, we can know only bit by bit over the course of time what God has placed in nature. As we learn, our conclusions and consequently our formulation of norms must change in response to new insights. In effect Janssens and others have moved the context for discovering God's will from the parentheses of the past to the horizon of the future.

The "past" is a collection of human knowledge regarding value, often preserved in the shorthand of normative statements. It derives from the historical journey of humanity in search of realities which embody value (goods). For those assuming a static world view this collection is reliable for its absolute nature, since

---

[76] "Historicity in Conjugal Morality: Evolution and Continuity," *Louvain Studies* 1 (1966-67) 267.

[77] Ibid.

[78] Ibid.

things do not change. For those embracing an evolutionary or historical world view the "past" is valid but insufficient, since there lies in the "future" the possibility of new values as well as new goods awaiting discovery. God is perceived as active in a real way in the time and space frame of existential reality. This perspective is acutely teleological, in that it reaches toward the future in search of a fulfilling terminus. This terminus, ultimately, is God.

Natural law, as participation in the being of God, is activity that is similar to God's activity. It is not a range of norms to be obeyed (Janssens' conclusion). [79] The normative given is the value and dignity of the human person. [80] The normative task is to transform nature into culture, or into what is suitable for service to humanity. [81] We deal with nature not arbitrarily but in a manner governed by proportionality. The moral agent is not free to tamper with or to thwart arbitrarily what is in nature, but only may intervene insofar as there exists a proportional reason which supports the actualization of a greater human value. [82]

Janssens locates the morality of the human act in the intention of the agent toward a particular end, which embraces whatever means are appropriate to it. This method of assessment of morality is not, however, the only approach found in the history of Roman Catholic tradition. In earlier times, as Janssens notes, particularly in the centuries which immediately preceded Thomas

[79] "Moderne situatie-ethiek in het licht van de klassieke leer over het geweten," p. 75.

[80] Janssens applies this norm to specific moral questions, especially in areas that confront the notion of biological finality. See, for example, the question of artificial insemination ("Artificial Insemination: Ethical Considerations," pp. 19-29); and use of birth control methods which interrupt the presumed biological teleology of sexual intercourse ("Historicity in Conjugal Morality: Evolution and Continuity," p. 267).

[81] "Historicity in Conjugal Morality: Evolution and Continuity," p. 267.

[82] See "Artificial Insemination: Ethical Considerations," p. 19. The question of proportionality will be examined in more detail in the next section on the principle of double effect.

Aquinas,[83] morality was taken to be the congruence between the act itself and its proper object. This same congruence characterized pre-Vatican II physicalism.[84] Janssens puts his own thinking in opposition to this method, which has recently been dubbed "Roman theology."[85] He speaks of importance in "Roman theology" of the *intention* of nature, which stands on its own outside the jurisdiction of the agent.[86]

An example which Janssens uses[87] will help to clarify this idea. In the Roman model the morality of giving food to the poor is derived primarily from the good object of the act itself. The motive of the agent, be it truly to help the poor or merely to look good in the sight of others or whatever, is of secondary[88] moral significance. As Janssens describes it:

> In short, there is first of all the natural goodness of all actions. On this essential basis moral good or evil occurs or supervenes (*accidunt*). With respect to morality, the object or matter of the action determines the *principal* morality (*bonitas vel malitia ex genere*) and the circumstances—under which head the end is also included—can add an *accidental* morality.[89]

---

[83] Janssens sees Thomas' approach as having moved to the position that Janssens takes. See "Saint Thomas Aquinas and the Question of Proportionality," p. 28.

[84] See discussion of the historical development which preceded Vatican II in Kelly, *The Emergence of Roman Catholic Medical Ethics in North America*, especially pp. 274-401.

[85] "Artificial Insemination: Ethical Considerations," p. 18. See McCormick's reference (1981) to Janssens's terminology in *Notes on Moral Theology: 1981-1984*, p. 50. By 1983 the term seems to be in more general use. Cf. Ibid., p. 171. This so-called "Roman theology" appears to repudiate the personalist thrust of Vatican II, demonstrated above.

[86] "Artificial Insemination: Ethical Considerations," p. 18.

[87] See "Saint Thomas Aquinas and the Question of Proportionality," p. 27. This discussion is derived from Janssens' treatment in the same article, especially pp. 26-28.

[88] Secondary here can mean either of lesser moral significance or even of negative moral significance when it is joined to action that is already designated as evil action.

[89] "Saint Thomas Aquinas and the Question of Proportionality," p. 27.

A comparative schema of the two approaches is helpful:
    Janssens' moral act:

intention (agent's*)—>end
(includes consideration of material,
volitional, circumstantial components)

"Roman" moral act:

intention (nature's [God's]**)—>object
end of the act as nature intends
(material component)

*seeks to respond in his/her openness to God
**self evident and/or elaborated by authority

A comparison between these two approaches gets at the
taproot of the disagreement over notions of intrinsic evil as well
as the assignment of this term to actions which are said to
frustrate the "natural" teleology of biological systems. Morality
which rests primarily on the act-object relationship must indeed
see intrinsic evil in any interruption of this connection.[90] Such an
interruption is particularly evident when it is demonstrated in the
concrete materiality of biological systems.

For Janssens, as for other personalist thinkers, the autonomy
and responsibility in freedom of the human person and the
achievement of the fullness of that human person rank above any
so-called moral laws in nature (physicalism).[91] As the norm and
end of morality, the human person must never be subordinated to
other norms, even as they appear to be expressed in an act-object
relationship. As Bernard Häring states:

[90] "Intrinsic evil" is taken to mean the material contents of the action. It does
not intend to express (as it does in some cases) a propositional statement in
language (norm) which includes *both* matter and intention. See Gula, pp. 56-57.

[91] Janssens does not, of course, abandon these laws altogether in his system.
He would, however, make distinctions between the universal relevance of values
and of norms. Cf. Vacek, "Proportionalism: One View of the Debate," p. 294.

A personalistic "natural law ethics" does not accept any taboo, since it does not adore created things. It is always a matter of understanding their final goal in view of the dignity of the persons and their relationship. Monotheism gives man a tremendous freedom toward the nonpersonal world, a responsible freedom which could never have become a common attitude under animism or pantheism. Man is called to shape the events, to transform the natural processes, and even to administrate his own biological and psychological heritage. The only moral limit is the dignity of every person and the building up of a brotherhood which as such gives honor to the Creator.[92]

Finally, the modern perception of the historicity of humanity and of creation itself does not affirm exact and fixed knowledge of God's imperatives nor the absolute character of norms derived from them. Janssens affirms that

[A] static conception of the natural law is not in keeping with the fact that the human person is a historical being (historicity), called throughout the course of history to transform nature into culture in the service of an existence worthy of man. In this perspective nature, both in and ouside of us, is rather the material which we must deal with in a human way. To recognize God's imperative will in this responsible task, we must always pose the question whether our actions are appropriate for the "person adequately considered" in himself and in his relations.[93]

Janssens, then, interprets natural law as the universal thrust of humanity toward congruence with the good, which good is articulated in and unfolded in the panorama of history. It is a position which affords the person a central place as value and as decision maker, situated above any principles of "nature." This position is consistent with the Roman Catholic tradition of teleology and with the personalist and historically conscious perspective of Vatican II.

---

[92] Bernard Häring, "Dynamism and Continuity in a Personalistic Approach to Natural Law," p. 206.

[93] "Artificial Insemination: Ethical Considerations," p. 20.

The Principle of the Double Effect

Introductory Remarks

Traditionally Roman Catholic moral theology has invoked the principle of double effect[94] as a method to deal with moral situations in which the outcome has more than one effect and the plural effects not all are good.[95]

Certain criteria[96] must be met:

In an act with more than one effect:

1) One may never perform an act
   a) that is intrinsically evil
   b) with a bad intention
   c) in a manner such that the good effect occurs directly consequent to the evil effect (evil as means to good)

2) There must be a "proportionate reason" for an action in which an evil effect is tolerated.

---

[94]Its modern formulation comes from the nineteenth century Jesuit, Jean Pierre Gury. See Jean Pierre Gury and Antonio Ballerini, *Compendium theologiae moralis*, 2 vols. 2nd. ed.: (Rome: Civilitas Catholica, 1869), p. 7, cited by Joseph Boyle, "The Principle of Double Effect: Good Actions Entangled in Evil," in *Moral Theology Today: Certitudes and Doubts* (St. Louis: Pope John Center, 1984) p. 259, n. 1.

[95] Knauer has suggested that the principle is much more broadly applicable. He has called it "the fundamental principle of all morality." See Peter Knauer, "The Hermeneutic Function of the Principle of Double Effect," *Readings*, 1, p. 1.

[96] On these four conditions, see, for example, O'Connell, *Principles for a Catholic Morality*, p. 171. O'Connell's formulation is fairly typical. Cf. Boyle, p. 244. Among the seminal articles reviewing the classic formulation of the principle, the most lucid is that of Peter Knauer, "The Hermeneutic Function of the Principle of Double Effect," *Readings 1*, pp. 1-39. See also J. T. Mangan, "An Historical Analysis of the Principle of Double Effect," *TS* 10 (1949) 41-61; J. Ghoos, "L'acte à double effet—Etude de théologie positive," *ETL* 27 (1951) 30-52 [a critique of Mangan]; Herbert G. Kramer, "The Indirect Voluntary or Voluntarium in Causa" (Ph.D dissertation, Washington: Catholic University of America, no. 42, 1935).

Distinctions Within the Principle

Intrinsically evil actions

First, an action may be designated as evil because it frustrates or goes against some natural tendency or teleology. This idea was discussed in the previous section: intrinsic evil is determined by the composition of the action (object) without regard to other elements. It is this understanding that grounds an act-object approach to morality and is the linchpin of deontological thinking.

Using this definition, most so-called revisionists[97] would deny that there are any examples in the set of intrinsically evil actions,[98] since for them morality can never be adjudicated without the consideration of additional elements. On the other hand, it would seem impossible to have an action that is "pure" in the sense of not producing some evil. Therefore clarification of the term "evil" is needed.

The tradition uses the term "evil" in the moral sense. Revisionists deny that any set of *actions* could be predesignated as immoral. They do, however, agree that there is a set of realities that embody significant disvalues, that is, certain actions may bring about material contents which include considerable ontic evil. Janssens maintains, that every action is mixed in its material contents. We are caught, as it were, in "the *simultaneous* and *inseparable* combination of good and evil, values and disvalues in our activity."[98]

Further, the tradition uses the term "evil" in an objective sense only. No matter how significant the evil material contents of an action are, one cannot infer subjective immorality without the assessment of how free and knowing the acting subject is in the

[97] This is the term applied to modern moral theologians whose methodology appears to transcend a strict interpretation of either deontology or consequentialism. It is synonymous with "mixed consequentialist" or "proportionalist" and conforms to Broad's "teleologist" The category includes McCormick, Knauer, Janssens, and others (Gula, pp. 61-79).

[98] "Ontic Good and Evil: Premoral Values and Disvalues," p. 67.

concrete deed. Indeed, Catholic tradition has held consistently that even the acting subject him/herself has only a reasonable certitude regarding the moral value of a specific action.

The tradition has also referred to "objective moral evil," that is, the *finis operis* has "an intersubjective moral meaning independent of the concrete intention of the agent and the consequences of the act."[99] Janssens, among others, does not agree with this definition, but defines a category he calls "ontic evil," which articulates the separation of the material components of the moral act from its properly moral ones. There are two aspects to Janssens' idea: on the one hand, ontic evil refers to the category of evil traditionally called "physical evil," that is, those categories of creation that in some way have a negative influence on human lives. Janssens states that it is not so much the reality itself that is evil, but that it *affects* humanity.[100] This sort of evil impacts from time to time on every human situation: from the virus that keeps a person in bed and away from work to the cataclysmic flood that destroys home and family, the community of humankind is affected by (ontic) evil.

"Earthquakes ... etc., are natural phenomena; but if they cause the death of human persons, demolish their homes, destroy their livestock and crops, then these *natural phenomena* which affect the lives and property of persons will be experienced as an evil and referred to as *natural catastrophes*." Janssens goes on to elaborate "what one designates as good and evil for persons or the human communities."[101]

Janssens wishes to expand the traditional category, however, to include the reality that is always present as a function of the human person as incarnate spirit or situated being. This expansion takes seriously the historic reality of humanity. Time and

[99] Albert DiIanni, "The Direct/Indirect Distinction in Morals," *Readings*, 1, p. 215.

[100] "Ontic Evil and Moral Evil," p. 133. Paul M. Quay recognizes this interpretation of Thomas as well. See "The Disvalue of Ontic Evil," n. 13, p. 265. In this article Quay attempts a direct negative critique of Janssens'proportionalist position.

[101] "Ontic Good and Evil: Premoral Values and Disvalues," p. 65.

space limit me.[102] My situation among others is a situation, as the Judaeo-Christian myth has long affirmed, "marked by sinfulness and by the results of sin."[103] These limitations *result* in ontic evil as a "natural consequence." Janssens insists that "limitation itself is not an evil."[104]

These limits render the moral agent unable to realize simultaneously the different values possible in a given moral situation. Every action will result objectively in a mixture of (ontic) good and evil. The agent must either refrain from acting at all and consequently remain unable to become what s/he is meant to be—an actualized human person—or act in such a manner as to accept the resultant mixture. The objective moral value of such action must be determined by distinguishing, as Janssens does, between what is simply *ontic* good or evil and what is the focus of the free intentionality of the person, *moral* good and evil.[105] This distinction is imperative in seeking an understanding of the difference between the act-object approach and the intention-end approach which Janssens takes.

It is clear that for Janssens (as he reads and agrees with the thinking of Thomas Aquinas) it is inaccurate to believe "that the material event of an act can be evaluated *morally* [emphasis mine] without consideration of the subject, of the inner act of the will or of the end."[106] To look at the exterior action without its human components (end and inner act of the will) is to consider only "an abstraction to which a moral evaluation cannot be applied."

[102] See above, especially pp. 67-70.

[103] "Ontic Good and Evil: Premoral Values and Disvalues," p. 63. At first there appears to be a coalescence between ontic and moral evil. This is true in one sense. What comes to this person, both from his/her own past human acts or from those of others, here and now comprises part of the real situation in which she finds him/herself and thus is part of the ontic reality or limitation in which the person must operate. As it is judged in itself (as human act), it is "moral." As it impacts on the concrete now, however, it is merely "ontic."

[104] "Ontic Evil and Moral Evil," p. 134. This point is missed by Quay, who insists that Janssens includes "also every creaturely limitation or mere absence of good that 'appears to the consciousness as a lack or a want' [quoting Janssens]" (p. 265).

[105] See "Ontic Good and Evil: Premoral Values and Disvalues," p. 69.

[106] "Ontic Evil and Moral Evil," p. 123.

Except in some theoretical sense one cannot speak of "objective *moral* evil," then, but only "objective *ontic* evil."

What does all this mean for human action? It means that no action I perform is without some evil, that is, some disvalue incorporated in an existential nexus of the real situation. Janssens does not mean to imply that human whim determines what is ontic evil.[107] As we saw above, anyone who is familiar with Janssens' work understands that he always sees the moral person as governed by objective standards. Our natural urge is to know and to move toward and to actualize what is of objective value. Our duty is to aim actions toward definite (ontic) good.[108]

The action choice to be made must take into consideration all the possible foreseeable (ontic) goods in this limited situation and fix the intention upon the actualization of some specifc value or values. Morality is determined by assessing the intention with these objective considerations. The means (the material component), part of the mixed object of the proposed action, must be evaluated proportionally, which is precisely the point which Peter Knauer makes.[109] Let us now turn specifically to a consideration of the intention.

With Bad Intention

On first glance it appears that this element can be dispatched quickly. As we noted above, few moralists would accept an action as moral if the intention is malicious, whatever else might be said. An intention to do evil vitiates any moral act, regardless of the plurality of consequences. Further, if the category of intrinsic evil is an empty set, unless one lists actions which by their linguistic specification *include* the element of intention,[110] the problem of

---

[107] This is Quay's incorrect reading of Janssens ("The Disvalue of Ontic Evil," p. 264).

[108] "Ontic Evil and Moral Evil," p. 116.

[109] See Knauer, pp. 10-14, especially.

[110] "Murder," for example, defines both a material component (killing) and a formal component (intention/attitude to malice).

intentionality is solved also. There is more to be considered, however.

In the descriptive sense, Catholic tradition has consistently affirmed that the human person psychologically seeks after the good.[111] While s/he may be confused or clouded as to whether this or that object is indeed good, s/he cannot, because of the natural teleology of the human faculties, seek evil as evil.[112] A "good" intention is, however, not sufficient to produce good action.[113] The agent must intend to conform his or her action to real good, that which embodies value, what Knauer calls "simply good"[114] and Janssens calls an object which embodies certain intrinsically desirable qualities.[115] For Janssens, the good inten-

---

[111] This axiom grounds the traditional Catholic criteria for judging morality from objective and subjective perspectives. On the one hand, morality may be judged objectively. Catholic moral theology has established three referents for objective judgment of the human moral act, the so-called "fonts" of morality: object, end, and circumstances (see O'Connell, *Principles for a Catholic Morality*, pp. 169-170. Cf. chapter two, and chapter three above). If all three are "good" (here we use the term in its ontic sense) the action is judged objectively "good," (that is, moral), and in a teleological system, right (cf. chapter three, part two).

As we saw in chapter three the "object" refers to the *external* result of moral action. The "end" refers to the intention of the agent as fixed on a real object.

"Circumstances" have been noted traditionally as elements which contribute to the objective moral meaning of an action. For Janssens, too, circumstances—in the form of the inescapable exigencies of a temporal-spatial existence—have their place in moral evaluation.

From the subjective perspective the judgment of moral conduct is made on the basis of the knowledge and freedom of the acting subject. If humankind is oriented to truth, s/he must know the truth in order to move toward it. If humankind must move toward truth to achieve his/her destiny, s/he must have the capacity (freedom) to do so. Therefore, impediments to knowledge (ignorance) and to freedom (passion, violence, fear, illness, habits of behavior or personality) mitigate the subjective responsibility for moral action. For an existentially oriented thinker like Janssens, moral action is always tinged with some limits.

[112] See Janssens' discussion of this point in "Saint Thomas Aquinas and the Question of Proportionality," p. 29.

[113] This is the major argument against Joseph Fletcher's situation ethics.

[114] Knauer, p. 2.

[115] See Janssens' definition of value in "Ontic Good and Evil: Premoral Values and Disvalues," p. 71; and "Geweten en zedelijke waarde," p. 439.

tion which flows from the enduring good disposition is the primary, but not the sole, seat of morality.

It will be helpful to review Janssens' construction of the human act, collecting the various terms used throughout his work and placing them in a semi-diagramatic form. While there appears to be some confusion and overlap of the meaning of some of the terms, especially in the Dutch, this diagram's use of the terms is consistent with Janssens' use throughout his work.

> The moral act begins in an
>> AIM (*streving* or *voluntas*)
>>> a potency

> which embraces the
>> END (*doel* or *intentio/electio*)
>>> [*finis operantis*]
>>> fixed on a real act

> which concludes in the existential reality the
>> OBJECT (*goed* or *actus exterior*)
>>> [*finis operis*]
>>> achieving real consequences[116]

For Janssens the final element both includes and actualizes the other two:

$$\text{AIM} + \text{END} + \text{OBJECT} = \text{one categorical reality}^{117}$$

---

[116] Since the *finis operis* for Janssens would be a mixed object (proportionate good/evil), including those consequences which are from causes other than that of the free causality of the agent, the "moral act" (including end, object, circumstances) is that placed intentionally by the agent. The consequences are ontic, but take on moral significance as embraced. They then become the agent's object (*finis operantis*) as well.

[117] See Janssens' comments on Thomas, "Ontic Evil and Moral Evil," p. 120. He notes that "the human act [although made up of both formal and material elements] is only one."

In other words the consequence is not only the external reality expressed in some real or material good (*finis operis*), but rather includes the actualized intent of the agent (*finis operantis*) which s/he had the potential to place (aim). What exists in reality is *not* several entities but a single entity viewed from different aspects. Essential to the consideration is the centrality of the intention-end equation. It is a frankly teleological approach to moral decision making, in that it observes the final complex event as its criterion for moral judgment, but it expands the teleological component to include the actualization of the intention of the agent. When all the elements are clearly good, as we noted above, it expresses an harmonious example of moral good as seen from the point of view of result.

How can we speak of voluntariness in the situation presented in the principle of double effect, however, namely a situation where *any* action produces a mixed object? The literature often frames the discussion in terms of the distinction between that which the agent wills voluntarily (and thus with moral implication) and that which is merely permitted. This distinction seeks to avoid linking the actualized intentionality of the agent with evil consequences. Janssens does not accept this distinction, since he sees "permission" as directed properly only toward an activity over which I have some degree of control. Actions which are the result of certain physical laws, over which I have no control, which stand outside me with their own causal systems, are not within the realm of my "permission."[118] Rather, such action constitutes a different species from moral activity, since truly moral action, says Janssens, flows from the freely aimed activity of an agent toward a chosen end.

The real question of intentionality from the moral point of view has to do with the vesting of love or malice (aim) in an act which is truly specific to the agent (end). If *the finis operis* (object) is to be embraced by the *finis operantis* (as Janssens, I think

[118] "Daden met meerdere gevolgen," *Collectanea Mechliniensia* 17 (1947) 622.

properly, affirms[119]), this identity in the moral sense has more to do with the agent's purpose (intention-end), the middle term above, than with a result that flows from physical causality (act-object). In the placing of an intention, however, the agent cannot elect just any action, but only an action suitable to the objective criteria.[120]

Yet, Janssens points out, often the relationship among the components of the action is so close that the effect of our free causality is created through the working of the necessary causality of the object. "Freedom and nature ... work together for one and the same consequence."[121] Therefore free action of the agent does not always mean free selection of or control over multiple consequences. This limited control does not, however, prevent the agent from freely willing a specific good consequence. Nor does it free him or her from the responsibility to seek more good than evil. Here Janssens is clearly not in favor of totally subjectivistic assessment of consequences: I feel good about this, therefore it is good. Causal responsibility is not always the same as moral responsibility. What constitutes the moral species of the action is the precipitate of love over malice (namely, the achievement of the value of the pre-moral attitude or motive which exists in potency and expressed concretely in the end on which the agent's intention is focused). This, in a sense, weights the total moral result of the action differently than if the action is done in malice, or for that matter, with little attention to motive or end.

This is Janssen's position. Since every action is mixed, affected as it is with the ontic components, morality is determined ultimately by the (objectively evaluated) end of the agent. It is this action, under the free choice of the actor, that is the subject for moral evaluation. Moreover, morality refers less to the individually placed act as such than to the overall development or

---

[119] Ibid. In his reading of Thomas, Janssens notes that for the scholastic thinker "the *finis operis* is always converted into a *finis operantis*" ("Ontic Evil and Moral Evil," p. 117). For Janssens the real result of action includes both the intentional and the proportionally chosen material component.

[120] Cf. "Ontic Evil and Moral Evil," p. 117.

[121] "Daden met meerdere gevolgen," p. 626.

blossoming of the person.[122] Personalist morality seeks not so much to tally a series of acts which are evaluated *outside the person* as objectively good, but rather to achieve persons who are objectively good. Another way to say this is that the person who is objectively good has actualized self by placing a consistent series of actions which flow from the attitude to do good and which objectively actualize value here and now. The actions themselves (in the sense of objective realities) are, in a sense, subordinate to the person (as self-fulfilling objective reality, Janssens' basic norm of morality).

The distinction between *voluntary in se* and *voluntarium in causa*[123] is really a distinction about how much the agent's intention (self) is invested in what portion of the effect. The loving intention[124] vests its energy and is congruent with the (ontic) good that can be done; the (properly proportionate and ontic) evil is regretted, though caused, by the agent, who does not invest his/her person (read self-creating intentionality) in this evil effect. While there may be two effects under an agent's efficient causality, these effects do not have the same relationship to the human person.[125] Direct and indirect causality, viewed from a personalist perspective, is concerned with how much the self is invested in the former and how little in the latter. Moral activity seeks for its primary end to bring about the fulfillment of the person in the image of God.[126]

---

[122] See Janssens' discussion on Aquinas' treatment, "Saint Thomas and the Question of Proportionality," p. 33.

[123] See Kramer's work, cited above.

[124] Janssens states, "In a positive way, since charity as *finis quo* is the final end of our moral life, the fundamental question concerning our actions has to be whether that which we do is able to be in the service of our love of God or to improve our relations with others and to society" ("Saint Thomas and the Question of Proportionality," p. 34).

[125] See discussion in "Daden met meerdere gevolgen," p. 631.

[126] Janssens has advanced this idea, as we saw in chapter two. Cf. Boyle, p. 251.

Evil As Means to Good

We must now address the question which was put aside in the discussion on intentionality above. In hybrid activity, a single action placed by a person may have its moral and physical causality so bound as to make it impossible to separate the two. A dilemma arises because the physical causality may produce effects which are not completely congruent with the moral causality of the agent.

We must make very careful distinctions here on the meaning of terms. To say that an evil effect produces a good effect is merely to indicate that what is here and now an evil objective reality (ontic evil) may be the causitive agent (means) in the production of good (ontic good [consequence]). To make this statement in the realm of being rather than in the realm of morality is to underline the obvious. In human acting there is always a mixture of good and evil present in the objective consequences. This good and evil must be designated ontic, however, until they are embraced by the human will.

It is here that we begin to find the contrast between Janssens' approach and some others. For Janssens, the various effects of actions are morally significant only if the agent's (objectively referred) self-actualization is vested in them. For others, if an effect flows from the direct action of the agent it is considered within his/her causal (include here moral) jurisdiction. A quote might help to clarify. Says Boyle: "In freely choosing to do something a person determines himself or herself to be a certain kind of person. For example, those who choose, however reluctantly, to end the life of an unborn baby by abortion make themselves killers, set themselves against life."[127] Boyle's measure for determining the moral species is weighted in favor of the characteristics of the material object (here designated as "intrinsic evil"), the death of the unborn baby. Intentionality ("make themselves killers") seems to be assessed entirely from those characteristics.

[127] Boyle, p. 251.

The action can be diagramed:

$$\text{intention} \longleftarrow \text{object (consequences)}$$
$$\text{means} \longrightarrow \text{good/evil object} \longrightarrow \text{good end}$$
$$\text{or}$$
$$\text{evil (as means)} \longrightarrow \text{good end}$$

(ACT RENDERED WRONG)

For Janssens, the flow is in the opposite direction:

$$\text{intention} \longrightarrow \text{end (includes consideration of}$$
$$\text{the object, i.e. consequences)}$$
$$\text{agent's end determines means} \longrightarrow \text{good}$$

$$\text{means} \longrightarrow \text{good/evil object} \longrightarrow \text{good end}$$
$$\text{(ontic components weighed proportionally)}$$

(ACT RENDERED RIGHT)

In the first diagram, no object is permitted which, flowing from the efficient causality of the agent, directly results in an (intrinsically, read: "morally") evil consequence. Such a consequence renders the action both potentially bad (subjectively immoral—assuming no impediments) and wrong (objectively immoral), since directly efficiently caused (moral) evil is considered to be wrong, and what is wrong (in the objective evaluation) cannot be done. This is a deontological argument. No "good" consequences can render the action morally good. Whatever values remain unactualized, the agent stands convicted of immoral action *because* of the nature of the exterior object under his/her direct efficient control (judged objectively evil). The emphasis is on the act-object relationship. Actions with mixed objects are allowed only if, in some fashion, the (objectively immoral) bad effect is secondary, that is, not the direct result of the agent's efficient causality. Therefore, in the classic example of the Fallopian tube pregnancy, the physician may excise the tube to cure an abnormal situation and save the life of the mother. The subsequent death of the fetus (which would render the act objectively immoral, if the death were caused directly) is considered not directly the result of the object (tubal excision), but a secondary consequence "permitted" in the total situation. A physician may not, on the other hand, crush the head of an infant lodged in the birth canal to save the life of the mother, since the good effect (saving the life) is the direct result of the crushing of the head (killing the baby—evil means).

In the second diagram the agent acts in congruence with a chosen end with proportional means (see section below). Although the result of his/her action may be mixed (ontic good and ontic evil) the morality is assessed according to the end (proportionally chosen and willed good) rather than according to the mixed object. A good end renders the action morally good. Ontically, the results are always mixed. In a teleological system, with morality evaluated on the basis of the totality of the action, there should be a congruence between the subjective good (the praiseworthy) and the objective good (the right), provided the agent's freedom and knowledge are not inhibited. Such inhibition would render an action subjectively moral but objectively immoral—if the latter term has any real meaning in the teleological system which Janssens espouses. The acting subject is required in every instance to include in moral evaluation *all* possible facets of reality. Ideally the resultant total object should be the best possible actualization of all those elements.

The distinction between "willed" and "permitted" is not made, in the same way as it is made in the act-object approach. That is, it is not made as a distinction of (physical) efficient causality, since the efficient causality of both objects (the realized motive and the realized material component) is that of the agent. The moral causality (the proportionally chosen end of the agent) could justify actions in both examples above. The physician in both cases intends to actualize (embody in real objects), insofar as possible, the value of human life. An evil effect, the death of a child, is part of the mixed object of his/her action in both cases.

Yet his evil effect remains outside his/her moral intention, while remaining within his/her efficient causality. As a moral intention, the distinction between "willed" and "permitted" makes sense. The agent intends to actualize the value of human life; s/he does not desire or delight in the death of the fetus. As efficient causality, however, the distinction is no longer the criterion for moral judgment.

Janssens' separation of moral and physical causality places the moral weight of an action within the subject, the human person as free positer of moral action. This idea is in line with the thinking of Vatican II, since the emphasis moves from the external object as the primary font of morality to the intentionality of the human person as this font. Says Janssens, "The principal distinction between classical notions and those of *Gaudium et Spes* is that the latter considers man's autonomy in an historical perspective."[128] An historical perspective acknowledges the imperfect nature of reality and places the burden on humankind to discover and to actualize the best proportion of good over evil by willed choice. It must be underlined, however, that with this shift in perspective Janssens never lets go of the objective criteria as important in the agent's process of moral decision making. How those objective criteria are weighed is next to be considered.

Proportionate Reason

It is essential to come to a clear understanding of the meaning of the term "proportionate reason." First, it can be taken to mean the subjective purpose or whim of the agent, disconnected from all objective criteria: if I feel strongly about a given action, that strength is proportionally greater than any dissuading reason. Grisez identifies this as the proportionalistic position and decries it because, "They [proportionalists—read: McCormick, Janssens, *et. al.*] are persuasive mainly because they agree with

[128] "Considerations on *Humanae Vitae*," *Louvain Studies* 2 (1968-69) 239.

prevalent secular humanism and appeal to everyone's desire to do as he or she pleases."[129] This, however is not Janssens' understanding of proportionate reason.

Second, proportionate reason can be interpreted as a weighing of benefits ("object" used in the narrower sense) over cost; good over evil consequences. Implied in this statement, however, is a circumscription of the set of benefits and harm to the *exclusion* of the actualized motive of the agent. This limits the consideration *solely* to a survey of the actualized effects, calculated in an almost mathematical manner. This is the position of the most crass utilitarians and is probably held by very few, if any, serious thinkers. If one reads proportionalism more carefully, it is clear that this is not the meaning of proportionate reason as used by Janssens and others.

Third, proportionate reason can be taken to mean the proportional relationship between the means and the end. It is this meaning that is found in Janssens' method. Let us review some of the distinctions from the previous chapter. For Janssens, the *agent* determines the end:

$$\text{intention} \longrightarrow \text{end}$$

and the end determines the means:

$$\text{means} \longleftarrow \text{end}$$

When the agent embraces the end, s/he must also embrace the material component (means) which serves as the vehicle to that end. Proportionality between the two is assessed in the choice of congruent means for a given purpose. It is not assessed *primarily* on the basis of the ontic good or evil of the means themselves. As Keane points out:

---

[129] Germain Grisez, *The Way of the Lord Jesus: Christian Moral Principles*, (Chicago: Franciscan Herald, 1983) p. 149. This is John Connery's objection as well. See "Catholic Ethics: Has the Norm for Rule-Making Changed?" *TS* 42 (1981) 232-250.

> A more adequate theology of proportionate reason asks what defines an action, what gives the action its meaning or *ratio*. It seeks after the intelligibility which informs the material elements of the action. If we simply add up the harms and benefits, we may fail to notice that a feature of the action which is mathematically on the smaller side of the scale is actually more central to the action, more definitive of what the action is ... proportionate reason cannot forget how the action is done, how the person wills it, or any other aspect of the action.[130]

The calculation does not negate the importance of the actualization of the motive of the agent. Thus proportionalism as defined by Janssens and others embraces the three elements in the circular diagram above.

It is the responsibility of the agent to determine with the utmost seriousness the means appropriate and proportional to his/her good end. If those means are frankly causitive of both evil and good, the means chosen must be productive of sufficient good (actualized value) to proportionally offset the evil (actualized disvalue). A trivial end (in which minimal value is actualized) does not support the use of dire means (in which maximal disvalue is actualized). To kill an unborn child to avoid the expanded waistline of pregnancy is not justified by proportionate reason.

In short, Janssens' emphasis in the consideration of the principle of double effect is the proportionality between means and end toward the actualization of the human person, the true constant norm of morality. What this means is deliciously simple: as a moral agent, I have an intention toward a particular end. Since my natural tendency is to seek to do good, I must ascertain that the good I seek conforms to real goodness. These objective qualities must weigh favorably against the disvalues embodied in the actual objects produced. I must assess my intention as to its goodness, since the actualization of the intention in itself is the actualization of a premoral formal value. Finally, I must, in the light of the end, choose appropriate means. That is to say, the

---

[130] Philip S. Keane, "The Objective Moral Order: Reflections on Recent Research," pp. 267-268.

means must be in proportion to that which I seek to do. Janssens' emphasis is consistent with the teachings of Vatican II and provides a nuancing of the principle of double effect which adequately reflects an historical world view.

Conclusion

We see in this examination of some specific points of Janssens' method a clear congruence to the moral methodology evident in Vatican II.[131] His focus on the human person, as the discover of value and the agent of self-actualization, is an historically based teleology. It locates the evaluation of morality in the concrete activity of the person. It finds the morally good, and therefore the right, in the real and intended actualization of value in situations which always exhibit limited possibilities for a mixture of good and evil. While respecting the natural teleology of the varied aspects of creation, Janssens' method, in keeping with *Gaudium et Spes*, places the value of the human person as the overarching consideration in moral evaluation. The human person, imaged from the divine template, must work out his/her destiny in the risky ground of becoming reality, where the absolute is to be discovered in the field of the future rather than in constants derived from the past.

---

[131] This congruence is not missed by Richard Gula, *Reason Informed by Faith*: *Foundations of Catholic Morality* (New York: Paulist Press, 1989) pp. 66-74. Gula elaborates Janssens' themes from his post-Vatican II English articles, rather than from the earlier French and Dutch material pre-dating the council, treated above (pp. 27-51). Cf. Dolores L. Christie, "The Moral Methodology of Louis Janssens" (Ph.D dissertation, Pittsburgh: Dusquesne University, 1988) pp. 93-94.

CHAPTER FIVE

TWO ISSUES

The previous chapters have investigated in detail Janssens'
personalist moral method, its roots, and its interface with certain
points of Roman Catholic moral tradition. In some work, especially during what we have called the middle period, Janssens
applied his personalist method to specific issues. In recent years
he has tended to concentrate on the elaboration of principles and
distinctions within the method rather than to treat individual
issues.[1] An examination of some specific applications will, however, prove useful - for example, human sexual activity, with the
emphasis on regulation of conception; and religious liberty, with
a focus on the interface between Janssens' thinking and that of
Vatican II. These issues impact on important moral questions in
the mainstream of twentieth century Roman Catholic moral

---

[1] Much of the specific work drew severe criticism from every one from the
pope to Janssens' theological confreres. With regard to the first, see "Address of
Pope Pius XII to the Seventh Hematological Congress in Rome, September,
1958," Odile M. Liebard, ed., *Official Catholic Teaching: Love and Sexuality*
(Wilmington: McGrath, 1978), nos. 785-786. Although the pope does not mention
Janssens by name, his choice of words ("Is it licit to impede ovulation by pills
...?") appears to be an allusion to the title of the 1958 article. The pope condemns
the work of "Some moralists [who] contend that it is permissible to take medicines
with this latter intention [to prevent pregnancy] . . . ." This oblique reference to
Janssens by the pope is noted in Noonan, pp. 554-555; and Swift, pp. 35-36.

With regard to the theological arena and reactions to Janssens' position see
Swift, especially pp. 22-48; and Grisez, *Contraception and the Natural Law*,
especially pp. 37-40; 157-167; and 172-177. Grisez's frequent sustained reference
to Janssens underlines how important the Flemish thinker's opinions were considered even by those who disagreed with him.

Even some of the groups which considered him their darling (the journal for
married couples, *Huwelijk en huisgezin* and the labor unions, for example) no
longer held him in such high esteem (interview with Jan Jans, 30 April, 1986). In
his later years Janssens has preferred to withdraw from such direct confrontations.
His later work, however, has served the useful purpose of refining his personalist
method.

theology. Since Janssens dealt with them for a sustained period of time, they demonstrate both his personalist method and development in his thinking. Moreover, Janssens' advances in these areas represent a significant contribution to Roman Catholic moral theology.

Human Sexuality

Background

It is helpful to recall the background to what became a major controversy in the Roman Catholic church. As early as the 1930's such prominent theologians as Heribert Doms and Dietrich von Hildebrand were laying the personalist foundation for a theology of marriage.[2] Their work moved discussion from a concentration on the *act* of marriage to an emphasis on the *meaning* of marriage. Mackin indicates that Hildebrand's work, in particular, "made a fundamental change in the very mode of thinking about marriage."[3] While Rome did not embrace the new ideas enthusiastically,[4] the seed for a new method of thinking had been planted. It would flourish in the years surrounding the Vatican Council.

As the council began it was hoped that some document would be included to change the ecclesial teaching on birth control. Instead, a papal commission was established to study the matter in detail. Paul VI's subsequent encyclical, *Humanae Vitae* (promulgated in July, 1968), rejected the report of the commission majority and reinforced previous teaching: no artificial barrier to the *act* of intercourse could be introduced morally to prevent

[2] See chapter one, pp. 15-16. Cf. Mackin, *What Is Marriage?*, pp. 225-231, especially.

[3] Mackin, *What is Marriage?*, p. 227.

[4] Doms' *The Meaning of Marriage* was withdrawn from publication more than two decades before the council by order of the Congregation of the Holy Office (Mackin, p. 225).

conception.[5] Further, the document included in its list of "artificial means" the newly developed progesterone ovulation inhibitors.

The Catholic community, newly vested with a Vatican II self image of confidence and personal responsibility, did not react to the encyclical with one affirming voice. Much negative response was forthcoming, especially in the United States. Even the American bishops responded to the ensuing dissent, with the pastoral letter, *Human Life in Our Day*, published November 15, 1968. Shortly before these events Janssens, animated by a fierce curiosity about the workings of God in the real world and urged by dialogue with married couples in his own country about their experience of marriage, began to develop new ideas of his own.

Janssens' Exposition

The Personalist Ground

Over several years Janssens's work has reflected and contributed to the discussion on human sexuality. His use of a personalist method provides an important ground for applied thinking. As Doms and Hildebrand had done, Janssens began to speak of marriage from the point of view of the human person rather than that of biology. This altered thrust is apparent in his work as early as 1952: "husband and wife form a community of life and love ...." "As a community of persons marriage has as [its] end the good of persons ..."[6] In works not specifically related to marriage Janssens explored the application of the connection between objective expression and subjective potential. He used the ongoing union of husband and wife to illustrate his position.

---

[5] An account of the workings of this committee can be found in Robert Kaiser, *The Politics of Sex and Religion: a Case Study in the Development of Doctrine, 1962-1984* (Kansas City: Leaven, 1985). He includes the text of the commission's final report. See pp. 248-263.

[6] "Huidige huwelijksproblemen," *Collectanea Mechliniensia* 22 (1952) 223, 222.

This relationship, he notes, flows from a disposition or attitude of benevolence toward the spouse (aim) which finds its actualization in concrete acts reciprocally given one to the another (intention realized in object). In this "communion of life and love" the spouses are able to make incarnate their love.[7]

We recall that for Janssens the pivotal value and starting point for any moral application is the human person, actualized in time and space. In application to marriage, this value is expressed concretely and dynamically in the fulfillment of the relationship between the spouses. The position is summarized in Janssens' 1969 article written as a response to *Humanae Vitae*:

> Marriage is, essentially and fundamentally, the communion of a couple in life and in love; it is because it is a covenant of love that Christ has called it to participate as a sacrament in his love for God's people. It is a covenant of *conjugal* love, a total commitment of the person of the partners, their wills, their affections, their bodies .... Conjugal love is a mission to be fulfilled: during the course of their life together, the couple devote their sustained effort to developing and perfecting their love, an unending task in the service of a *fundamental value*.[8]

Notice the hierarchy and progression of values here. The communion of the couple is the hinge on which the significance of marriage rests. Bodily expression of love (intercourse) is an essential *function* of this married love. Intercourse in turn finds its realization or full expression in children and in their upbringing. Since marriage exists in time and space, it must be actualized in real acts.[9] Its "mission" is to make perfect, to actualize this love. All other values are subordinate to this primary task. The other values of marriage articulate the *how* of its accomplishment. They

[7] See *Droits personnels et autorité*, especially p. 14. Here the French imitates the expression used earlier in the Dutch. Note that Janssens is true to his notion, discussed in the previous chapter, that concrete acts are secondary, contributing to the fullness of person.

[8] "Considerations on *Humanae Vitae*," p. 231.

[9] This idea is consistent with what has been said about Janssens above. See *Droits personnels et autorité*, p. 13, where he illustrates his method by application to marriage.

serve to actualize the primary value. These ideas are gradually developed and expanded in Janssens' work.

Development: Continuity and Change

Janssens sets out from his personalist base to pave the way for what in his thinking appears novel. He points to both continuity and change in the moral tradition of the Catholic church regarding marriage[10] and establishes his personalist application as part of this development. We can see this development from Janssens' vantage point, especially as it appears in the series of articles that began as a response to new chemical methods of birth regulation in 1958.[11]

In the earliest of these articles, a brief "note" on the morality of the inhibition of ovulation by chemical means, Janssens adheres closely to the previous orthodoxy, namely that procreation is the proper end of intercourse. He affirms the use of chemical

[10] This is precisely the point of his article "Historicity in Conjugal Morality: Evolution and Continuity," *Louvain Studies* 1 (1966-67) 262-268. This article, as noted in the introductory remarks, p. 262, is a translation from his book, *Mariage et fécondité* (Gembloux: Duculot, 1967), which revises and expands "Chasteté selon l'encyclique *Casti Connubii* et suivant la constitution pastorale *Gaudium et Spes*," *ETL* 42 (1966) 513-554.

[11] "L'inhibition de l'ovulation est-elle moralement licite?" *ETL* 34 (1958) 357-360 (published also in German as "Ist die Reglung der Ovulation sittlich erlaubt?" *Theologische Digest* 1 (1958) 248-251. This brief article was followed by two other articles in the same journal: "Morale conjugale et progestogènes," *ETL* 39 (1963) 787-826 (published also as J. Ferin and L. Janssens, "Progestogènes et morale conjugale," BETL, 22 [Louvain, 1963] 9-48); and "Chasteté conjugale selon l'encyclique *Casti Connubii* et suivant la constitution pastorale *Gaudium et Spes*," *ETL* 42 (1966): 513-554. The same thrust, sometimes expanded, sometimes truncated, and in some cases a translated rendering of the content of these articles, can be found in "Catholics and Non-Catholics: Their Collaboration on Family Planning," *World Justice* 5 (1963-64) 21-40; "Moral Problems Involved in Responsible Parenthood," *Louvain Studies* 1 (1966-67) 3-18; "Historicity in Conjugal Morality: Evolution and Continuity," *Louvain Studies* 1 (1966-67) 262-268. Finally there is the article in reaction to *Humanae Vitae*: "Considerations on Humanae Vitae," *Louvain Studies* 2 (1968-69) 231-253, which flows from the Dutch article, "Na *Humanae Vitae*," *Collectanea Mechliniensia* 53 (1968) 421-449. This list is representative of his work in the specific area of family planning. It does not exhaust the corpus, however.

intervention *only* if it can be justified by the conditions of the traditional double effect principle. One may use the new chemical means, for example, to correct pathology, to regulate the cycle, or to space children in imitation of "nature" for the purpose of promoting a greater number of children over a longer period of time. [12] His general conclusion is to accept the use of the then new methods *"when one intervenes to assist natural mechanisms which are defective or to correct pathologic situations."* [13] The intention directed toward a good end (assisting or correcting nature) allows the negative effects. These, though present in the totality of the external act, do not participate directly in the structure of the moral act as stipulated and placed. Janssens' statements represent a painstaking effort to affirm the tradition while leaving open the door to new technology.

In a second *Ephemerides* article (1963) he continues to situate his ideas within the panorama of historical development of new knowledge and new response. This position is consistent with Janssens' historical perspective treated above, which affirms the development of new values and moral insights based on the continual development of culture. In a meticulous examination of the history of the tradition on the regulation of birth and the theology of marriage, he traces real development, a departure from the monolithic position of Augustine.

For Augustine procreation is the biological end of intercourse and therefore the only reason for the marriage act. All other intercourse is at least venially sinful, including that performed to render the so-called debt of marriage, which serves to preserve one's partner from greater evil. To take pleasure in such a heinous although necessary act is sinful. [14] Janssens examines the dualism which he finds in Augustine's (and others') thinking, a dualism which separates effectively the biological from the spiritual. [15] For Augustine, notes Janssens, the best marriage is one in

[12] See pp. 359-360.
[13] Ibid., p. 359. Cf. Noonan, pp. 550, 553-554.
[14] "Morale conjugale et progestogène," p. 799.
[15] Ibid., pp. 800-803.

which the partners practice complete continence.[16] Among the scholastics Thomas follows the basic thrust of Augustine, with Albert the Great alone exhibiting a greater freedom in thinking.[17]

In this century we have affirmed the goodness of sexual pleasure and the rhythm method of spacing births. Janssens contends that the tradition thus shows a gradual rethinking of ecclesiastical positions, based on a richer understanding of biology and of the nature of marriage. When it was discovered that not every act of intercourse is a fertile act and the sperm alone is not the bearer of human life, it could be affirmed that intercourse at non-fertile times for reasons of the goods' of marriage (the Augustinian construct) is moral. Within the continuum of the past it is possible to offer new responses to developing knowledge.

Janssens shapes his argument regarding the use of progesterones to inhibit ovulation within this framework. He contends that the pill is a new development which must be addressed within the context of new knowledge about the biology of fertility. His position is that the pill is similar to rhythm, which places a temporal barrier[18] to the possibility of conception. The intention to prevent pregnancy is acted on by choosing to place an act of intercourse at infertile times. The pill allows the couple to do the same.[19] Neither periodic continence nor the pill interfere with the integrity of the marital act. Since modern biology has taught us that the human female is infertile *naturally* for all but a short period each month, infertility in itself ought not render an act unnatural, nor consequently, immoral.

For Janssens the factor that renders the marital act immoral is an ongoing selfish *attitude*, specified in intentional infertility.[20]

[16] Ibid., p. 803.

[17] Ibid., p. 799.

[18] This notion of time and of space, to which he refers in the article, will be further nuanced in the later "Ontic Evil and Moral Evil" article.

[19] See "Morale conjugale et progestogènes", p. 817. Cf. Swift, p. 27.

[20] See "Morale conjugale et progestogènes," p. 816; cf. "Catholics and Non-Catholics: Their Collaboration on Family Planning," p. 30. Note the shift from the consideration of the individual act of intercourse to the emphasis on marriage as a totality. The shift represents a turning point in the theology of marriage.

Any means to that end, barring interference with the natural act (later Janssens accepts such "interference"), are given their moral signification by the intention of the couple.[21] Only a global or complete intention to prevent the fruition of marriage is immoral. Such an intention would vitiate even those acts performed with means judged licit, such as periodic continence.[22]

This 1963 position appears very similar to that espoused by Doms and Hildebrand. There is a shift in emphasis or primary focus from the act of intercourse and its procreative function as the primary *end* of marriage to conjugal love as a value reflective of the *meaning* of marriage. Conjugal love in turn provides the nurturing environment necessary for the efficacious procreation and education of children.

The argument underlines the nature of conjugal love as the relationship between two human persons. The marital consent joins two persons to promote their mutual perfection in a unique and intimate union. This promotion must be in deeds not only in intentions.[23] Janssens states: "In sexual intercourse the mutual gift of bodies expresses and incarnates the abandonment of definitive and exclusive love. In effect, all true gift is definitive: we give away only that which we have ceded to the other."[24] This idea is key: if the "fundamental law of Christian ethics is the precept of charity towards our neighbor,"[25] the act of intercourse can be situated as the concrete expression[26] of this love in a

---

[21] This conclusion assumes the distinction seen above (chapter four) between the material components of a moral action and the intention. Refinement of this insight will come later, during the 1970's in Janssens' first ontic evil article.

[22] Cf. *Casti Connubii*, no. 84, which notes that periodic continence is licit for "mutual aid, cultivating of mutual love, and the quieting of concupiscence."

[23] These ideas are not new to the reader. We have examined them in the general treatment of Janssen's method above.

[24] Ibid., p. 810.

[25] "Catholics and Non-Catholics: Their Collaboration on Family Planning," p. 29. This article contains in English much of the content of the contemporaneous article in *Ephemerides*.

[26] Janssens calls it "intrinsically a specific expression of conjugal love" (ibid., p. 28).

married context. To vitiate this act is to act immorally. Over and above the use of contraception, vitiation can occur because of unreasonable or unloving demands made upon the spouse. Love that has as its main aim the egotistical or hedonistic satisfaction of a spouse or of the couple is not really love.

Even though there is this shift in emphasis regarding the purpose of marriage, Janssens asserts in 1963 that the marital act must be respected in its biological integrity and that contraceptive devices which interfere with this integrity are not moral. New technology allows Janssens to depart from Doms and Hildebrand in application of this thesis, however. The pill, since it provides no barrier to intercourse, is not a contraceptive and is therefore not included in the church's condemnation of contraception as against nature. "Indeed the success of *progestogenes* is largely due to the fact that they do not hinder total sexual relations."[27]

By 1966 Janssens has repudiated this position in favor of a more universal, if still tacit, approval of all contraceptive techniques in so-called "conflict situations."[28] Taking seriously the implications of his personalist method, he concludes that it is the right of the couple, in their attempt to realize the primary value of the total marriage, conjugal love, to find the means appropriate to safeguard and to promote this value. The complete structure of the act now is expressed not as a norm but as an ideal[29]—a shift from his earlier position.

Janssens, however never denies the importance of the procreative aspect of marriage. It is an integral part of the objective sense of the act of intercourse.[30] Yet, not "all the physiological

[27] "Morale conjugale et progestogénes," p. 822.

[28] See "Moral Problems Involved in Responsible Parenthood," p. 15. Janssens makes it very clear that such conflict situations are not exceptional. Early in the same article he has suggested that not many couples can practice total abstinence (p. 12) and that periodic continence and even the pill do not provide solutions for all cases (see pp. 12 and 14).

[29] Ibid., pp. 11, 17.

[30] See "Morale conjugale et progestogènes," p. 813. Cf. "Moral Problems Involved in Responsible Parenthood," p. 9.

possibilites have to be exploited."[31] Rather the couple is obligated to a balanced decision based on "a variety of obligations and a scale of values." They

> should exclude all egotistical motives and only admit objectively considered reasons and indications. Their reasons may be inherent in the claims of family life itself, or they may be extrinsic ones, due to the situations of society in the wider sense (demographic considerations on a regional or world scale).[32]

All of this argumentation serves to underline that Janssens' method places some values above those of biological integrity. At the same time, however, he nevers negates the importance of a generous fecundity to the centrality of marriage. He moves definitively beyond physicalism in asserting that the value of the marital act as procreative is subordinate to its value as community of persons.[33]

In the third article to appear in *Ephemerides* (1966) and in the expanded book (*Mariage et fécondité*, 1967) Janssens presents his thinking as harmonious with that of the council.[34] His argument for the personalist values of marriage as orthodox is made stronger by appeal to the personalist themes which he sees as central to the thinking of *Gaudium et Spes*. He quotes the council document to substantiate his own positions as consistent with the ongoing tradition and teaching of the church.[35] He postulates an

[31] "Catholics and Non-Catholics: Their Collaboration on Family Planning," p. 24.

[32] Ibid., p. 25. Cf. "Moral Problems Involved in Responsible Parenthood," pp. 9-10.

[33] Janssens is not the first to propose this theological advance. As early as 1965 the literature reflects opinions that abandon a physicalist approach. See Franz Böckle's survey of the contemporary European literature, "Birth Control," *Concilium*, 5: *Moral Problems and Christian Personalism* (New York: Paulist, 1965) pp. 121-129, especially.

[34] In commenting on Janssens's work of this period Robert H. Springer notes, "Whether or not one agrees with the Canon's well-known position on birth control—the acceptability of the pills and of other contraceptives in some circumstances—we cannot afford to ignore his reformulation of conjugal morality as a whole in a terminology closely approximating that of the Vatican Council," "Notes on Moral Theology," *TS* 28 (1967) 328.

[35] See especially "Historicity in Conjugal Morality: Evolution and Continuity," pp. 264-265.

objective norm which "lies in the totality of family and conjugal life, taking into account all the values involved in this totality itself and in its relations with other temporal communities—state and humanity—and the Church (no. 50)."[36]

At the publication of *Humanae Vitae*, Janssens reacts with vehemence, contending that the document ignores the personalist norm of *Gaudium et Spes* and replaces it with a strictly biological standard.[37] He sees a confusion in the encyclical between divine law (revelation ⇒ authority) and natural law (gradually discovered in the unfolding of history ⇒ autonomy).[38] In a reprise of the themes of autonomy and historicity that we have seen as central to his thinking, he repudiates the authority of the magisterium to establish universally valid norms.[39] He notes that

> such norms remain valid only as long as they continue to express the human values inherent in current historical acquisitions and possibilities. As soon as the magisterium makes a statement concerning concrete moral norms, it is placing itself within the domain of the legitimate autonomy of men and it is opening itself to dialogue with all men of good will (*Gaudium et Spes*, 33, 46).[40]

Summary

The linchpin of Janssens' argument throughout its development is the ultimate value of the human person as the norm of morality. In the case of marriage, the enduring community of life and love consitututes the norm that grounds the goods of marriage. Biological components are secondary to this value and can, under the category of means, be chosen in appropriate proportion to the intended end. Note that, as we stated above, Janssens never abandons either the tradition of the church regarding the value of married life and its consequences nor the essentially objective character of criteria for moral judgment. Finally Jans-

---

[36] Ibid., p. 265.
[37] See "Considerations on *Humanae Vitae*," p. 252.
[38] See discussion of natural law in chapter four, above.
[39] "Considerations on *Humanae Vitae*," pp. 244-245.
[40] "Considerations on *Humanae Vitae*," p. 244.

sens suggests that his position, which gives centrality to conjugal
love in marriage, is a recovery of the insight of Paul in scripture
that there is more to the marital act than simply its procreative
function.[41]

Critique

Perhaps more than anything else he has written, Janssens'
approach to the regulation of conception has been the subject of
discussion in the secondary literature, both scholarly and popular.[42] Much of the development and nuancing of his methodological thinking may be a response to the critique that followed
from his positions on birth control. This critique has taken two
directions. First, Janssens has been attacked from the point of
view of ecclesiastical authority. As his perspective is clarified and
as he stands in a different space from what appears to be the
concrete teaching of *Humanae Vitae*, it is not surprising that some
would find his positions troubling.[43]

While some theologians writing near the end of the council
supported Janssens' and others' assertion that the magisterial
treatment of family planning had evolved,[44] the reaction in the

[41] "Chasteté conjugale selon l'encyclique *Casti Connubii* et suivant la constitution pastorale *Gaudium et Spes*," p. 543. Janssens argues that Paul justifies
marriage for reasons other than procreation (1 Cor 7: 1-6). About procreation,
says Janssens, Paul "does not breathe a word" ("il ne souffle mot").

[42] The editorial note preceding "Ontic Evil and Moral Evil," p. 115, makes
this point, noting that his work on responsible parenthood was instrumental in
Janssens' appointment to the Papal Commission on Population, Family, and
Birth.

Much of the reaction to the second *Ephemerides* article is documented in
Louvain Studies by Francis Swift: "An Analysis of the American theological
reaction to Janssens' stand on The Pill,'" 1 (1966-67) 19-53.

[43] This reaction is aptly demonstrated by the comments of John C. Ford and
Gerald Kelly in the 1958 article, "Doctrinal Value and Interpretation of Papal
Teaching," Charles E. Curran and Richard A. McCormick, ed., *Readings in Moral
Theology*, 3: *the Magisterium and Morality*, (New York: Paulist Press, 1982) p. 10.

[44] See for example Franz Böckle, "Birth Control: A Survey of German,
French, and Dutch Literature on the Question of Birth Control," *Concilium*, 5:
Moral Problems and Christian Personalism (New York: Paulist, 1965) p. 105. He

United States both to his 1963 *Ephemerides* article and to his positions in general was swift and generally opposed.[45] Two key questions surface. First, was evolution both possible and demonstrable in the teaching of the church? To this question, as we have seen above, Janssens answers, "yes." He has tried to shape his own arguments within this development.[46]

The second question is more complex. It has to do with the proper jurisdiction of the ecclesial magisterium. Perhaps this question has more significance today, in questions dealing with family regulation, than it did in the sixties, where the optimistic assessment was that magisterial teaching was evolving into a more personalist stance.[47] Janssens' assertions regarding the proper place of the magisterium can be found in his response to *Humanae Vitae*. Its moral domain is:

1. To "define infallibly the existence of a real natural law."
2. To interpret infallibly "the contents of revelation on the subject of a christian moral way of life."
3. To "pronounce itself infallibly on theses which are so closely connected with revealed matter in the moral domain that they must be upheld in order to guard religiously and expound faithfully the content of revelation."[48]

notes that "even representatives of the Roman school see the norm no longer in the *actus per se aptus ad generationem et educationem*), but also in the *actus per se aptus ad mutuam donationem experimendum* (the act per se fitted to the expression of mutual giving.)"

[45] Much of this reaction is documented in Swift's article.

[46] See Böckle, p. 100. He documents and disagrees with those who suggest that Janssens' detailed examination of the tradition from the biblical period to the present day is brief and unqualified.

[47] The radical shift away from evolutionary opinion can be seen in several places. First, Joseph Selling has taken up Janssens' direction in suggesting that there is evolution, at least leading up to the 1980 synod on the family. See Joseph Selling, "A Closer Look at the Text of *Gaudium et Spes* on Marriage and the Family," *Bijdragen* 43 (1982) 30-48. Selling notes both the evolution of teaching which culminates in the council treatment (p. 34) and the reversion by the "Roman school" to pre-Vatican II interpretation (p. 40). While some have continued to appeal to Vatican II as novel and progressive, there have been others who affirm in the 1980's that there is nothing new in the teaching, that the "constant teaching" of the church does not change.

[48] "Considerations on *Humanae Vitae*," pp. 236-237.

If, as Catholic tradition has affirmed in its doctrine of natural law, morality is autonomous and does not depend essentially on the content of revelation to be known; and if, as Janssens and other modern theologians believe, morality is discovered gradually on the journey through the continuum of history, Christians, including the magisterium, are in dialogue with reality and with others in its discovery.[49] While it is the proper magisterial role to propose norms, based on the good of the community and the church's "vocation to be the living conscience of mankind,"[50] concrete moral norms may be proposed only in dialogue with others. Janssens' position, while logical and responsive to an historical world view and to the affirmation of the council about the autonomy of human conscience, has not been readily accepted by the magisterium.

Second, some have disagreed with Janssens from the methodological point of view. We find two levels of argument here. The first has to do with the importance of the integrity of the marital act[51] and represents a reaction to Janssens' earlier assertion that the pill does not destroy the integrity of the act but merely places a temporal barrier to fertilization. This early position assumes the essential moral significance of biological integrity and, in doing so, assumes the validity of a physicalist position with regard to natural law.[52]

The theological question centers then in whether or not the pill is an intentional interference with the natural act. If so, it is direct sterilization, an action the tradition considers morally evil. Lynch sums up the objection: "no euphemism of putting the ovary to

[49] We have discussed the relationship between the content of faith and the autonomy question above.

[50] "Considerations on *Humanae Vitae*," p. 242.

[51] In 1965 McCormick moves the question back one step. He insists that the discussion must first articulate precisely what constitutes a complete marital act. See *Notes on Moral Theology: 1965 through 1980*, pp. 47-48.

[52] As Dupré points out, this is one of the weak points in the early theological arguments in favor of the pill. See Louis Dupré, "Towards a Reexamination of the Catholic Position on Birth Control," *Crosscurrents* 14 (1964) 64; cited by Swift, p. 43. Grisez also finds the argument inconsistent. See *Contraception and the Natural Law*, p. 38.

rest can nullify the fact that oral contraceptives, when used as such, inhibit a natural generative function and make it at least temporarily impossible for a woman to conceive."[53] The thesis revisits the question of intrinsically evil actions. As Grisez points out in his 1964 book, "Yet it must be noticed that if the *individual acts* [emphasis mine] were not immoral, the decision to practice contraception could be precisely like the decision to practice rhythm."[54] Exactly! Since Janssens asserts (in his early argument) that the pill does not sterilize, but rather merely mimics a natural condition, he would see no difficulty in placing such an act.[55] In this assertion there lurks a tacit acceptance of physicalism and consequently of the category of intrinsic evil, a weakness Janssens corrects later. We noted this above.

Whether each individual marital act must be placed with an openness to conception is the point of disagreement here. Grisez's argument,[56] that the couple who practices rhythm need not intend this individual act, though placed at a hopefully infertile time, as contraceptive,[57] does not seem persuasive. Intention not to have a child is intention not to have a child. If my intention is to kill you, but, rather than hit you with an axe, I simply neglect to tell you that the glass from which you are about to drink contains poison, I am responsible for murder even though no act is placed. Omission is also grounds for moral responsibility. If I place a marital act knowingly with conception-preventing inten-

[53] John J. Lynch, "Notes on Moral Theology," *TS* 25 (1964) 244. Lynch's position is representative of the reaction that the 1963 article generated, particularly in the American theological community.

[54] *Contraception and the Natural Law*, p. 163.

[55] Janssens was not alone in holding this position. Böckle states, p. 119, "And I must admit that, presuming we take things seriously, there seems to be no serious ground for a significant moral difference between the two methods."

[56] *Contraception and the Natural Law*, pp. 160-163.

[57] This is precisely May's argument (pp. 103-104). Somehow he sees the means, contraception, as determinate of the intention not to have a child. That is, if a couple use a device to insure infertility in a given act, they are more surely intending not to have a child (contra-ception) than those who use a calendar (not a device?) to avoid conception in this particular placed act. The latter couple are "non-procreative" rather than "anti-procreative" (p. 104).

tion at an infertile time and neglect to place such acts at fertile times, my *intention* is contraceptive. The argument, sometimes proposed, that rhythm might not work and thus there is openness to God's plan is simply a testimony to my recklessness, not to my good intention. It may render the act less responsible but not less intentionally contraceptive.

The second level of reaction to Janssens' position concerns his more recent opinion, namely that the value of conjugal love is primary and that other values, including procreation and the biological integrity of the marital act, are in reality functions of that conjugal love, that marriage has an abiding meaning which at the same time transcends and expresses itself in procreation. The methodological insight which allowed and supported a shift in Janssens' thinking from concentration on the act itself as the primary seat of morality to the concentration on the value of conjugal love and especially on the *implications* of this new focus is possibly his most significant contribution to Roman Catholic moral method. It articulates the separation of the material components of the moral act from its properly moral ones. It is a shift that Doms and Hildebrand were unable to make. The insight that enables this shift to be made is Janssens' notion of ontic evil, which has been treated in the previous chapter.

Our natural urge, as we noted above, is to know and to move toward and then to actualize what is of objective value. Objective value in the case of marital decision-making is precisely the human person in his/her relationship of marriage. In the ideal case, the complex nexus of all values of married life are to be realized. Because of limitations that impact on the real situation of the marriage, however, the couple may find themselves unable in every case to actuate the totality of possible good: procreation, conjugal love, biological integrity of every married act. The action choice to be made must take into consideration all the possible goods in the limited situation and intend the best possible proportion of (ontic) good/evil. This intention, focused on the end, determines the morality. The means—the material component (even contraception, since it is a means, has no *moral* but only *ontic* connotation) are chosen in proportion to the end.

How Janssens treats this ontic aspect (the biological integrity of the marital act) changes over the years. In his early arguments, as we saw above, he proscribes interference with the biological integrity of the marital act. The pill offers an avenue around this difficulty. As his thinking changes, he begins to affirm at least tacitly that a couple could employ artificial means noting, "The ideal is, of course, that the married couple should always be able to realize the complete structure of the marriage act."[58] This statement seems to me to indicate that in 1966 Janssens still views interference with the biological integrity of the act as ontic evil.

By 1969 Janssens says little about the importance of the biological structure of the act itself. Following the personalist criterion established in *Gaudium et Spes*, he opts to affirm instead the "full sense of human procreation."[59] Both artificial means and periodic continence are viewed as "beneficial to responsible parenthood." In his first article on ontic evil (1972) he begins to illustrate the meaning of ontic evil by reference to Knauer's discussion of the question of birth control. Janssens agrees with Knauer's approach, citing the moral bond between the end and the means—in this case responsible parenthood and conjugal act.[60] He frames the question as the problem of "the relation of the *debita proportio* and ontic evil." Yet he stops short of calling artifical birth control ontic evil, shifting his discussion and application instead to the question of lying. By 1980 he has abandoned any preoccupation with ontic evil in the question of birth control and is concerned only with "whether or not an action is worthy of man or appropriate for the human person."[61] Any biological norm is subordinated to his primary and absolute norm: the human person adequately considered. It is difficult to conclude

[58] "Moral Problems Involved in Responsible Parenthood" (1966) p. 17.

[59] See "Considerations on *Humanae Vitae*," p. 241. Janssens draws upon *Gaudium et Spes*, 51.

[60] See "Ontic Evil and Moral Evil," pp. 143-144.

[61] "Artificial Insemination: Ethical Considerations," p. 21.

that Janssens would still speak of artificial birth control as "ontic evil."

The question of regulation of conception aptly demonstrates Janssens' moral method. It shows the development of his thinking in response to a particular concrete moral dilemma. This concrete example toghether with the exposition of his method in chapter three and the analysis of chapter four, give a clear picture both of Janssens' methodological insights and of their devlopment over time. A further example, this time in social ethics, will be offered in the following section.

Religious Freedom

Introduction

In the previous section we dealt with the application of Janssens' method to a question of individual ethics. Here we shall be concerned with a question of social ethics, that of religious liberty. While Janssens' has not limited himself to this issue in applying his thoughts to social ethics, the topic of religious liberty is an apt subject for exemplification. It illustrates clearly the expansion of Janssens' thinking, the interface with the developing doctrine of the church, and the specific personalist ground which Janssens' uses consistently and which the council embraces (especially in *Gaudium et Spes* and *Dignitatis Humanae*).

The tradition of the Catholic church with regard to freedom of conscience before the Second Vatican Council had been repressive, if not in practice, at least in theory. The beginning of the twentieth century found the church suspicious of modern ideas, including those of religious freedom. Curran observes, for example, that the position of Leo XIII on religious liberty, reactive to his era and its problems, is a negative one. Quoting Leo, Curran notes that "Liberty of worship goes against the 'chiefest and holiest human duty' demanding the worship of the one true God in the one true religion which can easily be recognized by its external signs."[62]

Further, "Those citizens who belong to other religions *do not have the right not to be prevented from professing these religions* ...." This statement reflects the comments in a pre-conciliar draft for the document on the church, presented to the perspective council participants in 1962.[63] Flowing from the premise that only the right has rights, oppression of members of religious traditions other than Christianity and specifically Roman Catholicism was not absent from the religious history of Western Europe. As the twentieth century approached its midpoint, however, the time was ripe for a new direction in Catholic thought. Popes from Leo onward began to express, at least tacitly and sometimes more overtly, an acceptance and endorsement of the idea of religious liberty.[64] This idea came to full flower in the conciliar document *Dignitatis Humanae*. After lengthy conciliar debate—the document on religious liberty was one of the last to be promulgated[65]—the council issued the historic treatise cementing a new development in Catholic teaching.

Janssens' Approach

Janssens was occupied with the question of the dignity of the human person as early as 1939 (*Personne et société*). The freedom of the situated human being is at the core of his method. The theme is expanded and nuanced throughout his work, taking center stage several times even before the council began their debate. In 1954, his *Droits personnels et autorité* dealt briefly with

[62] *Directions in Catholic Social Ethics* (Notre Dame: University Press, 1985) p. 7.

[63] See Pietro Pavan, "Declaration on Religious Freedom," *Commentary on the Documents of Vatican II*, 4, ed., Herbert Vorgrimler (New York: Herder and Herder, 1969) p. 50.

[64] David Hollenbach documents this gradual change that characterizes the twentieth century. See *Claims in Conflict: Retrieving and Renewing the Catholic Human Rights Tradition* (New York: Paulist, 1979), chapter two.

[65] In December, 1965.

the question of religious liberty in connection with the person's relationship to societal institutions and jurisdiction. The purpose of organized society, the common good, is to provide for the greatest possible flowering or blossoming of the subjective culture of each of the citizens.[66] It is the free and knowing choice of each person that determines ultimately who s/he will properly become (subjective culture).[67] The task of the society is to protect and to enhance the free exercise of this becoming[68] and to intervene only in such a way as to groom this skill. This theme is the same as that in his magister thesis and his 1957 book (*Personalisme en democratisering*) and is reprised in *Freedom of Conscience and Religious Freedom*[69] and elsewhere.

Janssens' position on religious liberty is illustrative of his personalism. Beginning with his magister thesis, Janssens insists on the origin of the rights of human beings in the dignity of the human person as a unique, conscious, free, and responsible being.[70] These rights are not granted by the state or through social contract (as marxist or liberal systems affirm), but are proper to the human being as s/he is. They include the right to life, health, and choice of vocation; the right to personal conviction, opinion, and conscience; and the right to organize in communities which promote the subjective culture of each human person.[71] The rights of the human person are inalienable and independent. They have bearing on the objective sense of the person and on his/her reality as a self-creating situated subject. They are essential for the person to attain his/her personal destiny. What flows from the person as a right provokes a corresponding duty. The social implication of individual "right" is the "duty" of the society and of other persons to avoid

66 See *Droits personnels et autorité*, p. 17.

67 Ibid., p. 19. Cf. *Freedom of Conscience and Religious Freedom*, p. 108.

68 *Droits personnels et autorité*, p. 21.

69 See p. 55.

70 See chapter two, above.

71 See "Rechten van de mens" (1952), pp. 529-532; and *Droits personnels et autorité* (1954), pp. 47-48. Cf. "World Justice," *World Justice* 1 (1959-60) 29 ff., which contains some of the same themes in a slightly different format.

impediments to the exercise of the rights. For Janssens the notion of "right" goes further, as we shall see, to include not only this negative understanding (freedom from impediment) but a positive understanding. The latter implies a duty of society to assist the person not only in the pursuit of, but also in the exercise and implementation of this right. The dialectic relationship between the subjective and objective cultures illustrates this.

These human rights are not without limitation. On the one hand, the real situation of the person can be a limiting factor. My talents and my choices constitute an inner barrier to the free rein of my right.[72] If I am short, I am unlikely to be able to exercise my "right" to a vocation in the National Basketball Association. If I choose to smoke two packs of cigarettes a day, my right to health is likely to be threatened. On the other hand, limits to my rights may be imposed from without. First, the particular place in which humanity finds itself on the continuum of time and history limits me to the actualization of the values possible at this point in time. Second, society may impose external limits upon the individual for the common good, that is, to protect from abuse, to insure collaboration of persons, and to promote the objective culture.

For Janssens the right to freedom of religion flows from the inalienable right of the human person to freedom of conscience. The most basic aspect of freedom of conscience, and indeed of the human person, is the right to pursue one's destiny, that is, the relationship which is union with God. Without the freedom to do this, the human person cannot perform this duty or destiny as a truly "human act," that is, an act which stems from freedom and knowledge.

Janssens delineates three principles applicable to freedom of religion. First, there must be as much freedom as possible for the individual and for the group to pursue their religious destiny.[73]

[72] See "Rechten van de mens," pp. 536-539; "The Rights of the Person," *American College Bulletin* 38 (1959) 116-121 (a translation from *Personalisme en democratisering* [1957]); and *Droits personnels et autorité*, pp. 56-64.

[73] *Freedom of Conscience and Religious Freedom* ,p. 82. The idea of specifically religious liberty is expanded in the detailed book prepared before the council

Because the human person is a moral subject and because moral subjectivity is dependent upon freedom, the person must not be impeded in his/her freedom, even in the case of an erroneous conscience. Says Janssens:

> Raised to the dignity of a moral subject, the human person is able to pursue his moral perfection only by assuming the responsibility of conforming his free acts to the judgment of his conscience. He still enriches this moral perfection even if, in spite of the care which he devotes to the search for truth, he forms and follows an erroneous conscience. In this case he still actually desires moral good and he perfects himself by acting out of love for this good. [74]

This position is not one of indifferentism or individualism. It is based on the premise that persons naturally seek the good and can accomplish this task only if they do so freely. Further, because the person is an open reality, fundamentally present to and in dialogue with the persons and things outside him/herself, he or she must always take into consideration the objective realities as they exist when making moral choices.

Second, in the proper exercise of authority, legislators may impact on the freedom of persons only as is absolutely necessary. Janssens gives the example of the right of a society to legislate school attendance. This legislation protects children from the abuse of parents who may not wish to educate their children. A government may not, however, dictate totally what kind of education should occur (for example, indoctrination in conflict with parental beliefs) but must allow as much freedom as possible within its law.

---

completed its consideration of the topic. His book is a masterpiece of harmony, weaving as it does the (then) recent papal utterances about the traditional position of Roman Catholicism that certain rights are inalienable into the fabric of his own personalist thinking (see pp. 7-8). The primary connection from the tradition deals with the question of freedom of conscience. For Janssens, freedom of religion is the extension and application to the question of religious freedom. He even draws from some of the ostensibly repressive papal statements of the last century to see a kernel of possiblity for a modern doctrine of religious freedom (see, for example, pp. 21-23).

[74] Ibid., p.81.

Third, society must be responsible for the common good. Janssens elaborates three elements of the common good: coexistence, collaboration, and coparticipation.[75] The modern era has witnessed a gradual shrinking of the barriers between ourselves and people of other cultures and ideologies. Peaceful coexistence on a global level in today's world, says Janssens, "is a question of life or death."[76] Dialogue with others underlines both our basic equality as moral subjects and our basic originality, which works itself out in the unique set of values actualized in each of different cultures. We, especially because of our Christian perspective, are called to treat all people as others like ourselves, that is, to value them in love and to call them from their error, if any. If others do not accept that which we believe, however, tolerance must characterize our behavior toward them.[77] This tolerance must be embodied in objective elements, in our actual behavior toward others.

With regard to collaboration, Janssens calls upon his model of the dialectic relationship between the subjective and objective culture. Collaboration, as "a constitutive element of the common good must be imposed, even if for that purpose some restrictions in the exercise of freedom of conscience prove to be necessary."[78] Coparticipation has to do with the requirements of distributive justice. All persons in a society are entitled to share in the fruits of that culture. All of these elements have implications, says Janssens, for the question of religious freedom.

With coexistence comes the need to recognize that faith is both free gift of God and free response by the person. This realization

[75] These elements are applied in detail to religious liberty in Janssens' book. We can see them already a part of Janssens' thinking in earlier works, however. See "Recht and moraal" (1956) pp. 523-530; and *Personalisme en democratisering* (1957) pp. 62-63. They are mirrored in ecclesiastical teachings as well. See, for example *Pacem in Terris* (1963), in Joseph Gremillion, *The Gospel of Peace and Justice: Catholic Social Teaching since Pope John* (New York: Orbis Books, 1976) pp. 12, 13, 31, and 34.

[76] *Freedom of Conscience and Religious Freedom*, p. 84.

[77] Ibid., pp. 90-91.

[78] *Freedom of Conscience and Religious Freedom*, p. 105.

must govern the attitude taken toward those who do not believe as we do. "A faith imposed by compulsion is, therefore, a contradiction in terms ...."[79] Yet Janssens insists that such benevolent toleration does not mean we affirm relativism. Rather, the "revealed doctrine" about the free nature of faith forms the basis of our toleration.

Catholics are called to collaborate with others in their mutual task of actuating the best possibilities of culture. Because we, created in God's image, share his creative work, and because we are called to love others, we are expected to collaborate in this mutual project. This task is ultimately governed by moral norms.[80] The primary constraint on collaboration for Catholics is that they be "able to remain themselves, that is, safeguard their religious life and accomplish their apostolic mission."[81] Janssens summarizes: "In all cases Catholics can never forget that their faith and their charity oblige them to participate in collaboration, but also to invent modalities and different methods for a loyal and fruitful contribution."[82]

In contrast to the repressive positions of earlier times (naught but truth has rights) Janssens insists that the principle of coparticipation demands the opposite response. He states that "truth has no rights,"[83] but rather carries with it obligations "to conform our conscience to the requirements of objective truth." The privilege of the "truth" of faith, then, is to "defend and promote the good of *human persons*." Coparticipation in as much freedom as possible is the right of persons in a society, and this right must be protected and enabled by the governing structure of the society.

---

[79] Ibid., p. 123.

[80] Janssens roots moral norms that govern cultural development in the natural law, which he notes is "what is demanded by the dignity of the human person" (ibid., p. 126).

[81] Ibid. The subjective culture, in this case the subjective religious culture, is always the starting point for development of the objective culture.

[82] Ibid., p. 130.

[83] Ibid., p. 131.

Thus we see that the "common good" as a goal for a society is grounded in a personalist perspective. The good of individuals within the society is the corrective and balance in achieving the "common" good of all citizens. As much as possible religious freedom of coexistent, collaborative, coparticipant people must be provided over and against the needs of the common good.

Catholic Tradition on Religious Liberty

Janssens' positions on religious liberty are certainly congruent with Catholic tradition on the human person. The extension of this idea into the realm of religious liberty has been particularly apt in this century. The twentieth century has been faced with the breakdown of traditional pockets of like-minded people as well as with the gradual introduction of the value of personal liberty that was heralded in the revolutions in France and the United States in the eighteenth century.

Let us look more closely at the tradition. As David Hollenbach points out, the cornerstone of the Catholic rights theory is the dignity of the human person. "The thread that ties all these documents [the last hundred years of Catholic social teaching] together is their common concern for the protection of the dignity of the human person."[84] This thread can be demonstrated beginning with the social teaching of Leo XIII (d. 1903). Hollenbach notes:

> Leo's encyclicals laid the groundwork for the modern Catholic theory of human rights. Human dignity is the foundation of this theory. The defense of dignity was the source of his objections to the liberal theory of the state and its overriding concern with the preservation of liberty negatively understood.[85]

[84] Hollenbach, p. 42.

[85] *Claims*, p. 49. Leo's distrust of the liberal tradition made him suspicious of such concepts as religious freedom and equality. Leo states that one of the chief duties of the state is "to favor religion, to protect it, to shield it under the credit and sanction of the laws, and neither to organize nor enact any measure that may compromise its safety" (*Immortale Dei*, in *Great Encyclicals*, p. 111). Leo's notion of freedom in this regard applied only to "true religion," however, not to "errors" such as liberalism.

As Leo spoke out against the abuses to labor that were current in his time, he affirmed the right to food, clothing, shelter, formation of unions, and a living wage. Yet his model for social organization continued to be hierarchical,[86] with the concept of religious liberty seen as "anathema."[87] His world view could not go beyond the princes and powers that provided the necessary stabilizing glue for the nineteenth century model states of Europe. The experience of the French revolution, characterized by its poor treatment of the institution of religion, and other threats to the model seemed merely to strenghen his belief.[88]

Pius XI (d. 1939) spoke more generously of "true freedom of conscience," especially as an argument against the totalitarian regimes that dotted Europe in the 1930's.[89] His meaning of the term, however, while it included the elements of rights, dignity, and freedom, still reflected the hierarchical and classical view of society which he had inherited from the past.[90]

During the era of Pius XII (d. 1958), the dignity of the human person took center stage as the principle by which government authority was interpreted. The government now is pictured as "defending the rights of human beings and of promoting the freedom of the people."[91] The use of the term *principes*, favored

[86] See, for example, Leo's treatment of the hierarchy of laws (*Libertas Praestantissimum*, pp. 140-142). All law, even human law, is seen as rooted in the divine law. Cf. Hollenbach, pp. 48-49 and Curran, p.12.

[87] Curran, p. 13.

[88] Curran notes that Leo viewed the liberal tradition that found its expression in the French revolution as the cause of "all the problems of the modern day. Liberalism substitutes foolish license for true liberty" (p. 8).

[89] Curran, p. 11. It is clear that for Pius XI the idea of freedom of religion applied only to those who practiced Christianity. In *Divini Redemptoris*, for example, in which he specifically attacks communism, he notes that "the Papacy has continued faithfully to protect the sanctuary of the Christian religion ...." See *Divini Redemptoris*, in *Sixteen Encyclicals of Pope Pius XI* (Washington: National Catholic Welfare Conference, 1937) p. 5. There is no question of the same protection for other faiths.

Recall that it is during this time that Janssens' work, *Personne et société*, appeared. It, too, spoke at great length about the human person in relationship to the state. Cf. Hollenbach, p. 53.

[90] See Curran, p. 11; and Hollenbach, p. 56.

[91] Curran, p. 12. Cf. Hollenbach, pp. 56-61.

by Leo, drops from the papal vocabulary to be replaced by more collegial language.

In the work of John XXIII (d. 1963) the notion of freedom of religion becomes explicit. From *Mater et Magistra* to *Pacem in Terris* John adds "freedom" to his list of truth, justice, and love as the ground of human dignity.[92] Governments are now viewed as protectors of the rights of citizens. This is a far different starting point from that of Leo. Religious rights are specified. John states: "Every human being has the right to honor God according to the dictates of an upright conscience, and the right to profess his religion privately and publicly."[93].

Declaration on Religious Liberty

As noted above, the Second Vatican Council was the occasion for the promulgation of religious liberty as an explicit teaching of the church. Starting life as an appendage to another document, *Dignitatis Humanae* became a separate entity, as the result of a long process of deliberation within the council. The question initially was treated as a part (Chapter Five) of the Decree on Ecumenism.[94] This first schema was presented to the council on November 19, 1963. After a series of revisions (the final schema was the sixth), during which the document came to stand as an entity in its own right, the Declaration on Religious Freedom was passed and promulgated in the ninth public session (December 1965). It was heralded as "perhaps the greatest and most characteristic progress achieved by the Council."[95]

Let us outline briefly the major points made by the document. First, the document grounds its development of understanding[96]

[92] Curran, p. 13.

[93] *Pacem in Terris* in Gremillion, p. 14.

[94] Pavan, p. 51. From this point to the final schema approved by the council members, the person most notably involved with the schema was the bishop of Bruges, E. J. M. de Smedt, a man closely connected with Janssens ecclesially and theologically.

[95] Pavan, p. 62. He quotes from a contemporary Italian article.

[96] It is interesting to note, as does Abbott, p. 677, n. 4, that this is the only conciliar document that indicates explicitly that its intent is to *develop* doctrine.

"on the inviolable rights of the human person and on the constitutional order of society."[97] Flowing from the dignity of the human person as endowed by God with reason and freedom, which we know through both revelation and reason, each person must be protected from coercion to act against his/her beliefs or to act in accord with the beliefs of others.[98] In the "internal, voluntary, and free acts" proper to humanity, the person, discovering "ever increasingly the unchanging truth" of God's law, proceeds "with prudence [to] form for himself right and true judgments of conscience, with the use of all suitable means." These means include, because of the societal nature of humanity, "the aid of teaching or instruction, communication, and dialogue."[99] Human social nature requires external acts, including religious exercise in community, which acts must be shown "favor" by government and not inhibited.[100]

The document argues that within an organized society all religious groups have the right not to be hindered by the state in the exercise of self-government, the choice and training of ministers, and the public teaching and witness to their proper belief.[101] This right to free pursuit of religion extends to the family.[102] While it is the right of a government to regulate in some ways the conduct of its citizens, this regulation must be in conformity to the objective moral order,[103] which exists to safeguard the rights of citizens and to solve problems that arise from conflicts of rights. Finally, the goal of religious freedom is that people "may come to act with greater responsibility in fulfilling their duties in community life."[104]

Although this principle seems to be operative elsewhere in official council documents (the personalist thrust of *Gaudium et Spes*, discussed above, for example) and is an important thesis in Janssens' position on the morality of progesterones, it is not invoked specifically by the council in another document.

[97] Abbott, *Dignitatis Humanae*, 1.
[98] Ibid., 2.
[99] Ibid., 3.
[100] Ibid.
[101] Ibid., 4.
[102] Ibid., 5.
[103] Ibid., 7.
[104] Ibid., 8.

In the second chapter the question of religious freedom is explored more specifically in terms of its connection to revelation. Whereas chapter one focused on the argument from reason, here the concentration is on the Christian perspective. The act of faith is "of its very nature a free act"[105] exemplified best in the being and work of Jesus, who did not force the acceptance of his message, but offered the gift of faith in freedom.[106] While acknowledging the presence and power of government, he worked outside its framework, as did his followers.[107] The church is called to follow this example and expects that she, too, will be granted reciprocal freedom in her relationships with government and with the whole civil order.[108]

The final portion of the document calls the faithful to form their consciences by careful attention "to the sacred and certain doctrine of the Church."[109] It emphasizes the need for the right to religious freedom to be incorporated in the constitutions of governments, noting that in some cases this right has not been granted.[110] The decree cites the increased closeness among the people of the modern world that characterizes this century.

Interface: Janssens and Tradition

The conclusions of the council on the question of religious liberty are drawn from the same wells that Janssens uses in establishing his position.[111] Catholic social ethics has its roots in

[105] Ibid., 9.

[106] Ibid., 11.

[107] Ibid.

[108] Ibid., 13. This is considered one of the key points of the document (see p. 693, n. 53).

[109] Ibid., 14.

[110] Ibid., 15.

[111] Jans has suggested a much stronger connection. In a recent article he proposes a direct link between the original pre-conciliar committee on the question of religious freedom and Janssens' thought. At the first meeting of this committee a short text, *The Freedom of Religion*, was offered for consideration. It was this text, according to Jans, that set the direction for the later conciliar declaration.

Jans asserts that both Bishop De Smedt, who was so involved with the document at the council (cf. Pavan, pp. 51-61), and Janssens himself affirm the

the developed teaching of the church on the dignity and rights of human persons.[112] This differs from liberalist and marxist traditions in that the distribution of rights to persons is not dependent on human decision, either by contract or by governmental imposition. Rooted in the natural law tradition, Catholicism has affirmed that human dignity is a self-evident concept, able to be known to all. As Hollenbach notes:

> The reality of human dignity and its structure do not depend for their existence upon the knowledge or recognition of human agents. However, precisely as images of God, human persons do in fact have the ability to know and respect the dimensions of human dignity in at least an imperfect way.[113]

Janssens' work is compatible with the development of the Catholic tradition in this century, as we have seen. He too roots his conclusion that people should enjoy freedom of religion in the dignity of the human person. For Janssens, the content of natural law in this regard is precisely what is worthy of the human person, what best promotes his or her development as a person.[114] This content is discovered on the human journey by the open free conscious human person.[115]

Both Janssens and Catholic teaching draw upon the themes of Christian revelation. The assertion that humanity is made in the image of God and that human dignity befits that image is a theme found both in Janssens and in the council document. Revelation grounds the activity of the human person to seek the truth in freedom and the freedom from coercion that must accompany that search.

It is of note that both Janssens' work and that of official

---

latter's authorship of the early document. In Janssens' opinion, says Jans, "this text was the most important thing he ever wrote." See Jan Jans, "Some Remarks on the Work of Professor Emeritus Louis Janssens," in *Personalist Morals*, pp. 324-325.

[112] The origins and development of a Catholic theory of rights can be found in Hollenbach, especially chapter two.

[113] Ibid., p. 117.

[114] See *Freedom of Conscience and Religious Freedom*, p. 40.

[115] Cf. *Dignitatis Humanae*, 2.

Catholic tradition beginning in the 1960's (John XXIII and *Dignitatis Humanae*) are historically conscious.[116] Beginning with this period, official magisterial teaching in social issues takes on a more and more inductive, or historically responsive methodology.[117] We have seen this insight to be a general and persistent theme of Janssens' thinking. Built on his methodological ground, the human person as a pilgrim on the journey through time and space, every social application of Janssens' method considers the historical aspect.

Finally, both the Catholic tradition and Janssens are concerned with the social dimension of humankind, especially in a world in which cosmopolitan cultures and values interface. This interface demands a dialogue, a toleration, and a system organized to safeguard the rights of all in the exercise of religion. This protection is the proper function of the civil government, whose jurisdiction is precisely the common good.

While we shall not attempt here to demonstate direct dependence on the work of Janssens, the themes of the twentieth century social teaching of the Catholic church and those of Janssens are remarkably similar. The importance of the human person and the shift to an historically conscious position are essential to both. The possibility that doctrine can develop and that new ideas can be incorporated into teaching as they are

---

[116] See Pavan, pp. 63-64, in this regard. One of the difficulties of the council was to resolve the blatant dichotomy between the position of Leo XIII on religious liberty and the "new" insights of the mid-twentieth century. The solution chosen was to emphasize the evolutionary nature of implications of the teaching about the dignity of human persons. As the teaching evolves it includes gradually a greater sphere of rights in response to the historical reality in which it finds itself. This is precisely Janssens' idea: new situations provide new possiblities of values, which must be dealt with. These new values are then incorportated into the objective culture.

This is the same approach we have seen in Janssens' treatment of the previous question, that of conception regulation. The congruence between Janssens' position and that of the official magisterium in regard to that question, at least in recent documents, has not been so clear.

[117] See Curran's comments on the work of John Paul II, for example, pp. 32-36.

encountered is overt in Janssens earlier than it is in church teaching. The latter makes it explicit in Vatican II.

In sum, Janssens' method as applied to the question of religious liberty reflects his major insights. The dignity of the human person is the ground and norm of human rights. Since the human being is an open, free and consicous being, he or she must be allowed to exercise this freedom in the most fundamental aspect of existence: the search and actualization of human destiny in relationship with God, freedom of conscience. This personalist ground is congruent with the development in Catholic thought that has characterized the latter half of the twentieth century.

Further, in order to provide a method which moves beyond the moral field of the single individual to that of the person in relationship, Janssens applies his basic theme of the interplay between the subjective and objective cultures. In the case of the question of religious freedom, he uses the terms and their implication to speak of the subjective and objective *religious* cultures. His themes of coexistence, collaboration, and coparticipation, as applied in the area of religion, are principles which govern the tension between the good, in this case religious, of the person and that of the corporate whole, the state (the common good). "As much freedom as possible," the norm which guides the application of the principles in society, is based in Janssens' most fundamental norm: the human person adequately considered.

CHAPTER SIX

FINALLY CONSIDERED

In the preceding chapters we have explicated in detail Janssens' moral methodology, noting its philosophical roots and historical development, underlining its major personalist themes, and exploring its interface with the theological tradition of Roman Catholicism. A consideration of two moral issues illustrated the application of his method to both individual and social ethics as well as the development of his thinking.

The keystone of the method is the human person adequately considered. As we saw above, Janssens affirms the human person adequately considered as the sole and absolute norm of his methodology. It is the basis for both the theory and the application of his method. It is set forth as the criterion for morally right action. Let us consider the adequacy of this assertion.

An Adequate Consideration?

Richard McCormick, whose *Notes on Moral Theology* have done much to introduce Janssens to the English-speaking reader, thinks that the norm is adequate. He argues that Thomas Aquinas' position, "we do not wrong God unless we wrong our own good,"[1] is equivalent to Janssens' criterion. Janssens' criterion situates the moral project not in a vertical dimension (God ⟷ humanity) but in a horizontal dimension (humanity ⟷ humanity). The question is, however, more complex. We must uncover what constitutes the human person adequately

---

[1] McCormick translation. See *Notes on Moral Theology: 1981-1984*, p. 51. The citation is from *Summa contra gentiles*, 3, 122 ("Non enim Deus a nobis offenditur nisi ex eo quod contra nostrum bonum agimus").

considered, who is the assessor of adequacy, and what are the implications of the answers to these questions?

As to the first, Janssens tells us repeatedly that the human person is a free and knowing bodily subject directed toward relationships with others, the world, and God. This complex structure situates the human person in an objective context for moral evaluation. Moral choices are not made merely on the basis of a single criterion such as the bodily specificity of the person (physicalism) nor on the way the agent feels about this or that act (subjectivism). Moral decisions must be submitted to a norm whose contents are both objective and inclusive. The norm is judged adequate insofar as it is meets these criteria. Perhaps the personalist criterion, although the starting point is different, is ultimately the same as the traditional dictum attributed to Augustine, "Love God and do as you please." Assumed in this statement is that in the love of God is to be found the call to love self and others; therefore it becomes an inclusive rather than an exclusive dictum. This is true as well for the personalist criterion: to value the human person adequately considered above all else is to find and to value others and God.

The human person, adequately considered, is neither an individualist nor a subjectivist category.[2] As Selling has noted in his comments on Janssens' insights, we do not speak of "this human person, or that one, not me or you, not us or them, but *the* human person."[3] The content of the human person adequately considered is, therefore, beyond the narrow vision that this individual person might conceive: it is an objective category. We must add that *the* human person is a developing reality, so its

---

[2] This point is affirmed by McCormick. He states: "sorting out the claims of conflicting values is a community task subject to objective criteria. Because the individual must make such assessments at times does not mean that the assessment is correct *just because the individual has made it.* Thus, it is not proportionate to kill another just because I mistakenly believe it is" (*Notes on Moral Theology: 1965-1980*, p. 699). Cf. *Notes on Moral Theology: 1981-1984*, p. 113.

Janssens' personalism is not subjectivistic, even though it does emphasize the importance of the human person.

[3] Joseph Selling, personal letter October 11, 1987.

contents may not be the same yesterday as today, today as tomorrow.

How is the content of the human person adequately considered to be decided? This is a problem that is addressed obliquely in much of the critique of Janssens' method. Those critical of Janssens tend to call upon the need for "objective standards" in moral evaluation. I offer as example Quay's accusation that revisionist thinkers do not use "consistent conceptual categories."[4] Quay's (and others') discomfort may be rooted in the desire for the authoritative categories that have dominated some previous methods and which impart a sense of security to the decision-making process.

McCormick, too, comments that such discussions often dissolve into questions about authority. It appears easy, safe, and even appropriate to find an external authority to define or to validate certain actions as moral or immoral. The avoided alternative is to decide for ourselves what this content shall be. Perhaps this alternative is rejected initially because we are awed— and rightly so—with the responsibility demanded by the admonition to follow conscience. As Josef Fuchs notes, "The function of conscience is to help man, as agent, make his action authentic (i.e., self-realizing)."[5] Ultimately, Janssen's personalist method demands what scripture models[6] and traditional teachings have affirmed:[7] that conscience is the final proximate (subjective) norm of morality. Ultimately conscience is the determinant of what is of value and how it is appropriated in the decision-making context. We saw this as a central part of Janssens' method (chapter three). Ultimately it is I alone, the subject standing

---

[4] "The Disvalue of Ontic Evil," p. 262.

[5] See "The Absoluteness of Moral Terms," p. 109.

[6] I offer as example the Lucan story of the prodigal son and loving father (Luke 15: 11-31). As a model of the divine paternity, the father in the story neither preaches nor forces.

[7] See O'Connell, *Principles for a Catholic Morality*, pp. 91-93, for example; or James P. Hanigan, *As I Have Loved You: the Challenge of Christian Ethics* (New York: Paulist Press, 1986) pp. 120-124.

before the present reality, who must evaluate, decide, and choose the *content* of the moral norm here and now.

The result of these choices is the self creation of the human person by the human person. From this viewpoint, as Norbert Rigali notes, "Living becomes analogous to creating a work of art, and moral law is seen as the most authentically human historical design that can be created out of the present material of reality."[8] As I bring myself to being, I am both artisan and artifact.

Second, let us turn to specific problems with Janssens as a proportionalist. As McCormick notes, proportionalism, or the notion of proportionate reason, plays "an utterly crucial role in Janssens' thought."[9] As we examine the relationship between the subjective and objective components, we recall that traditional theology has spoken of objective moral evil. As we noted above, this category is valid in Janssens' method only insofar as it defines two aspects, that is, it includes both formal and material components. For Janssens it is an invalid category if its contents include only those items which are descriptive of material evil. He defines material evil as ontic.

Yet, moral evaluation can never deny the categories of morally right and morally wrong action. For Janssens, the morally right is determined by values, both formal and material, that are actualized in the consequences. Moral rightness cannot be determined by the material component of the action alone. Morally right actions are those in which one or more values worthy of the human person, in dialogue with objective reality, are selected for actualization. This is the goal for which the "good" person strives, as McCormick notes.[10] The means, as proportional to the end (in reference to the value or values selected), are assessed as well. Therefore, proportionalism is a teleological method of doing

[8] Norbert J. Rigali, "Morality and Historical Consciousness," *Chicago Studies* 18 (1979) 166.

[9] *Notes on Moral Theology: 1965-1980*, p. 695.

[10] *Notes on Moral Theology: 1981-1984*, p. 113.

ethics that focuses on the relationship[11] between the end (chosen to actuate the agent's intention) and the means (ontic component utilized to achieve the end sought). The morally right is judged objectively from the results of human action.

Proportionalism has been analysed both by those who agree with it and by those who do not. A particularly helpful schema is proposed by Lisa Sowle Cahill, who poses four questions to clarify the discussion.[12] First, does proportionalism say that the end can justify the means? As we have seen, and Cahill agrees, in one sense the answer is "yes." Proportionalism advocates the choice of a means proportional to an end, by which the person seeks to actualize a particular value or values. Its relative status as (in some cases) ontic evil (Cahill's phrase: "a departure from the ideal fulfillment of human nature")[13] must be evaluated within this formula. Proportionalism does not advocate embracing moral evil.[14]

Moral evil, we recall, is evaluated in Janssens' method in the teleological context: proportionate (ontic) good/evil consequences and good motive actualized in those consequences. Moral evil in Janssens' method is either intentional malice (desiring or wishing [intention] to do evil)[14]) and/or the choice of proportionate ontic evil/good (more disvalues than values actualized; disproportion between [ontically evil] means/[ontically good] end) in the consequences. To embrace moral evil is to act in an objectively morally wrong manner.

If the agent is impaired in some fashion (lacking knowledge or freedom), the action is not judged subjectively immoral but may be judged objectively *wrong*. That is, as seen from outside the

---

[11] Curran uses the phrase "reciprocal causality" to refer to the relationship between the formal and material components in Jasssens' method. See "Utilitarianism and Consequentialism: Situating the Debates," *Louvain Studies* 6 (1976-77) 250.

[12] See "Contemporary Challenges to Exceptionless Moral Norms," *Moral Theology Today: Certitudes and Doubts*, pp. 121-135.

[13] Cahill, p. 128.

[14] See Ontic Good and Evil: "Premoral Values and Disvalues," pp. 62-63, on the distinction between benevolenie and beneficience.

perspective of the person, it lacks the criteria for moral rightness. I suggest that one cannot say that the action is objectively *immoral*, however, since the category "moral" can be applied only to persons, not to realities apart from persons. To make this distinction is to understand and to apply Janssens' ontic good and evil insight.

Since proportionalism does not advocate the embrace of moral evil, the answer to the question is as Cahill notes, "no." A morally evil means is not justified by a (morally or ontically) good end. For Janssens, however, a means can only be judged "morally evil" retrospectively, if it is disproportionate to the end, unless, of course, the means is defined in such a manner as to include something which is formally evil, that is, evil formally intended.[15]

Second, Cahill asks: "Is this theory the equivalent of 'utilitarianism' or 'consequentialism'?" She distinguishes between what she calls the utilitarian version of teleology, which sees as "end" the greatest good for the greatest number, and the position held by many modern Catholic proportionalists. Those in the latter category, which includes Janssens, are not content with a finite good (as are Cahill's utilitarians), but rather define good in a transcendent sense. Transcendent good, as in Janssens' system, does not exclude certain minorities (lesser number) from its calculation or from the distribution of good consequences. The norm of the human person, adequately considered, demands equal status for each, as we saw above in the second section of chapter five and elsewhere. The goal of the common good (objective culture) is the individual good of each person (subjec-

---

[15] Murder (malicious killing), for example, as a means, would render an act immoral, even if the consequences were proportionally good. Janssens makes the following distinction: "If ontic evil is *per se* intended, the end itself (the object of the inner act of the will) is morally bad and, being the formal element (reason and cause of the external action), vitiates the entire action" ("Ontic Evil and Moral Evil," p. 140). Killing (regretted but proportional taking of life) as a means (not an end in itself), may be part of a moral act, provided the consequences are proportionally good. I hasten to add that Janssens would not advocate wholesale killing in any case.

tive culture). Further, the theistic base of Janssens' method demands that each person be treated fairly, since every person is an image of God. For Janssens, as we saw above, the transcendent, and specifically the theistic element, is essential. It is applied in the absolute norm: the human person adequately considered.

Third, Cahill asks whether proportionalism is too difficult, too tenuous, or too ambitious a tool for moral evaluation. This question is similar to that raised by Ramsey,[16] and others: how does one weigh the relative merit of values, and so forth, in a given moral decision? Ramsey thinks "that the class name *proportionate* will become adequately informative only when it is fully spelled out which evils are greater than the merely great, which goods greater than the lesser, what values override what other values in case of clash, and so on."[17] Janssens has answered this objection in detail in "Norms and Priorities in a Love Ethics."[18] He refers those who would use proportionate reason to the order of charity and the order of good. In the order of charity (*ordo caritatis*) each person must be looked upon with equality and impartiallity. Yet, since each is original and unique, the demands of charity do not require necessarily *equal* treatment, but rather *appropriate* treatment, that is, attention corresponding to the special needs of each. Expanded into the social realm, this demands — familiar themes from chapter five — co-existence, collaboration, and co-participation in the interchange between the objective and subjective cultures.

In the order of good (*ordo bonorum*), beginning with the moral goodness of the human person as absolute value, he suggests several criteria for deciding among conflicting or competing lesser values in a given moral situation: 1) values are not equal; priority ought be given to the higher value, 2) the urgency of the value

[16] See Paul Ramsey, "Incommensurability and Indeterminancy in Moral Choice," in Richard A. McCormick and Paul Ramsey, ed., *Doing Evil to Achieve Good: Moral Choice in Conflict Situations*, (Chicago: Loyola University, 1978), chapter three.

[17] Ibid., p. 124.

[18] We draw from pp. 219-230.

should be taken into account, 3) the degree of probability for actualization should be considered (a more possible lower value may be chosen over a less possible higher value), 4) ordinarily, long term values ought not be sacrificed for short term values (e.g., neglect of sleep, etc. for the sake of furthering one's profession, may end up sacrificing [through illness] the value sought [the profession] in the long run), 5) values which protect social life (institutional values, for example) ought to be paid special attention. Finally, he offers prudence and the continued practice of moral goodness as suggestive of "the greatest chance to comply with the demands of priorities" in concrete situations.[19]

While this catalogue offers some answer to Ramsey's objections, it is still virtually impossible to foresee all the implications of every possible choice in a given moral dilemma. Teleologists are correct to point out that (strict) deontologists are often equally unable to justify the rules and duties on which they base their system, especially as these are specified and applied in complex concrete cases. This is precisely the conundrum posed by the limited reality to which humanity is heir.

A different objection in this context is one raised by Albert DiIanni, namely that of the *serial* nature of the moral act itself.[20] In a rather interesting presentation DiIanni shapes the argument in terms of the consecutive moments in a moral action.[21] Looking at the structure of the moral act in much the same way we treated it in chapter three above, DiIanni sees:

$$\text{aim} \longrightarrow \text{means} \longrightarrow \text{end}^{22}$$

---

[19] Ibid., p. 230.

[20] "The Direct/Indirect in Morals," p. 222.

[21] McCormick has commented in detail on this article (ibid., pp. 713-717). He moves in a slightly direct direction, however.

[22] Cf. Janssens' approach, treated in chapter three:

$$\text{aim} \longrightarrow \text{end}$$
$$\text{means} \longleftarrow \text{end.}$$

The example he uses is familiar (taking a fetal life to save a mother):

| causal aim————————→homicide————————————→death |
| (agent intends) | (*finis operis*) | (ontic result) |
| | [moral action] | [in itself] |

The question he asks is: is it formally immoral (evil intention aimed at homicide) to aim directly at a non-moral evil (death)? He appears to agree with Janssens' thesis, that the *finis operis* and the *finis operantis* come together in the human action. In fact, this is precisely the point that he finds troubling.[23] The way in which these elements intersect for the two thinkers is different, however. For Janssens the *finis operis* is taken up into the *finis operantis*. The agent assents in his/her act to the precipitation of a particular reality, even when faced with the knowledge that this reality may be a mixture of actualized (ontic) good and evil. The careful agent knows, perhaps better than those who are not thoughtful in moral deliberation, that every human action is mixed. In order to achieve the ontically good result, s/he must absorb this mixed result in the totality of the action. The intention is directly aimed at the good result, however, and the evil result is regretted. In the case of the example given, the one death, weighed against the alternative (two deaths), seems to be proportionate, that is, there is greater ontic good than ontic evil in the result.

This is not DiIanni's approach. He understands the *finis operantis* as aimed directly at the death of the fetus (*finis operis* = homicide) to be the substantial moral act. Thus for him the *finis*

---

[23] In this I presume he affirms Grisez's position: one may never act directly against one of the basic human goods. Says Grisez: "One about to choose in a morally right way respects equally all of the basic human goods and listens equally to all of the appeals they make through the principles of practical thinking" (*Christian Moral Principles*, p. 197). All basic human goods must "be realized and protected." None of them may be slighted "for the sake of another good which will thereby be possible." Cf. discussion in Gula, pp. 82-83; cf. McCormick, *Notes on Moral Theology 1965-1980*, pp. 701-702. McCormick discusses this point with regard to May and Grisez.

operantis dissolves into the *finis operis*. What he calls the non-moral result (death of fetus to save mother) is for DiIanni *beyond* the moral consideration, if I understand his argument correctly. It remains "simply the immediate effect of the act."[24] I see two problems with DiIanni's analysis. First, he constructs the moral act in such a way as to present a difficulty that reverses that of Ramsey. Ramsey cites the impossibility of knowing and sorting all the projected consequences of a given action; DiIanni circum-scribes the moral act to exclude anything other than the imme-diate and direct (what I would term "ontic") result of the agent's *causality* (not defined as the agent's *end*).

Let us answer this first objection by recalling the meaning of moral action in Janssens' method. Moral action is that which produces moral persons.[25] For Janssens, moral persons are those who place their actions consistently from an attitude to do good in the ontically mixed situations in which they find themselves. To disconnect their moral evaluation from all but the existentially immediate object is to make the human person less than the visionary and architect of future possibilities that s/he is. It is to minimize the intentional element in such a manner as to delimit the scope and real meaning of human knowledge and freedom. It is to deny the definition of human being as image of God and co-creator.

The second problem raised by DiIanni's definition concerns the primary site of morality. If I limit the content of moral action to an intention fixed on a material object in itself, unqualified and unsituated—dissected, as it were, from its existential moorings—I return to a non-personalist methodogy, one which attaches moral implication to the material content *as primary*. Since DiIanni wants to call such an action "intrinsically evil in a weaker sense than that of the manual tradition,"[26] a "lesser moral evil" which

[24] DiIanni, p. 222.

[25] See pp. 154 and 207 above. Janssens' concern is with the subject as free, knowing responsible actor. These characteristics demand that the person own, insofar as it is possible, the exigencies of the real situation.

[26] DiIanni, p. 222.

ought evoke moral guilt and what he terms "creative regret," I think this is precisely what he does. As we have seen above, however, for Janssens an action does not become moral until and unless the agent's intention is specified in connection with a given end. The "end" considered merely as "object" in itself has no intrinsic moral significance. In the example DiIanni gives, the agent appears to desire as *end* the death of the fetus. S/he apparently wills this consequence *qua* end. For Janssens the death of the fetus is viewed quite differently. It is seen rather as a (proportionate) *means*, albeit a regretted and reluctantly chosen means, to the end (actualizing as much life as possible) in a difficult and mixed context. To view this situation with regret, even DiIanni's "creative regret," it is not necessary to impute a "minimum moral index." [27] An action is adjudicated to be either moral or immoral. It is neither adjudicated outside its ontic components nor bound completely by their implications. It is not partially immoral, although it can produce partially (ontic) evil results. Janssens would agree with DiIanni that "if the good end sought could be achieved in some other way which avoids [this evil] and produces at least an equal amount of good this other must be done." [28] This is precisely the meaning of proportionalism.

Janssens would agree that it is immoral to aim directly at a non-moral evil *in itself*. He would define the action differently, however. For Janssens the subject aims not at death *per se*, but rather at realizing the value of life, in this case proportionately more life than would have been possible without some action. Janssens takes seriously the responsibility of the subject to act or not to act. He does not abdicate personal responsibility simply because the case is difficult because of its potentially mixed result. In this example, not to act would result in a greater (ontic) evil: the death of both mother and child. Not to act in such a case, allowing both mother and child to perish, would seem to be worthy of blame, therefore immoral.

[27] Ibid., p. 224.
[28] Ibid.

DiIanni affirms that the person who would kill the fetus to save the mother is likely to suffer feelings of guilt. It is essential to distinguish between moral guilt and the feelings of guilt that flow from other sources. If I kill a person because the brakes fail on a borrowed automobile, I feel regret, perhaps even guilt. Yet clearly I have no *moral* responsibility for the action. If I do not have moral responsibility, I cannot be morally guilty. As McCormick points out,[29] though, Janssens is among those who affirm (with DiIanni) that one ought to feel regret for such action, *even though it is not immoral.*

Cahill muses that moral objectivity must not be confused with simplicity. Our investigation of Janssens would affirm the truth of this statement. Yet, the moral project is essential to humankind and must be embraced.

Fourth, she asks if the method is defined with sufficient precision. This question is not unique to Cahill, but has been raised by Quay and others as well. In chapters three and four we have tried to solve some of these problems with respect to Janssens, namely the distinction between the physical act and the moral act and the place of circumstances. The relationship between act and circumstances for Janssens is an essential distinction for the definition of the moral and the ontic components. Circumstances constitute the concrete temporal and spatial elements that limit the complete actualization of all that is theoretically possible in any moral action. They describe the concrete possibilities and circumscribe the set of concrete means available here and now to actualize those possibilities.

One concept Cahill thinks needs clarification is "value term."[30] Quay has found difficulty with Janssens in this regard. He [Quay] sees a lack of clarity in Janssens' attempt to differentiate between the terms "value" and "good." Says Quay: "In brief, Janssens' 'ontic evil' is simply equivalent to 'negative value' or disvalue.'"[31]

[29] Ibid., p. 715.

[30] McCormick uses this phrase to get at the confusion between the material and formal content question (see *Notes on Moral Theology: 1981-84*, p. 64).

[31] Quay, "The Disvalue of Ontic Evil," p. 265. Quay insists on offering his own definition: "a privation of good that is proper to or called for by the natural

This is not an accurate reading of Janssens. Janssens sees value as a formal concept until such time as it is embodied in a real object as a good.[32] Quay's is an easy mistake to make, if one's knowledge of the Flemish thinker is limited to the (sometimes inadequate) English translations of his work.[33] The careful distinctions between good and value are much clearer in some earlier material written in Janssens' first language[34]. In this earlier material the distinction between these terms is quite clear, contrary to what Quay affirms.[35] The distinction is crucial, since one cannot deny the importance of values inferred in human actions. Yet at the same time, as we have seen, one cannot always actualize (convert into "goods") all the values possible theoretically in a given instance.

Quay's argument implies much the same thing. He affirms that human moral action is "free moral choice among limited goods and under the limitations of material world."[36] Where Quay and Janssens seem to differ, however, is in the nature of the duty that a human person has to avoid actualizing (ontic) evil. For Quay such evil refers to "a privation of a good called for"[37] and appears to impose upon the agent a duty to avoid causing it.

Janssens' designation of ontic good and evil are probably more precise than such terms as pre-moral good and evil, since they make it clear that the material components are not of themselves morally conclusive.[38] Quay himself notes that "without the inclu-

integrity of a being or its mode of acting" (p. 267, n. 17). In doing so, he comes close to locking in the agent to an ought based on nature.

[32] Quay appears to hold the same definition. See "Morality by a Calculation of Values," *Readings*, 1, especially pp. 271-272.

[33] As more of Janssens' work has been translated into English by those who know his method, this has become a less severe problem. In this decade some of Janssens' work has been written in English.

[34] See above, chapter three.

[35] Janssens' second article on ontic evil was an attempt at further clarification, particularly in light of Quay's objections, as we noted above.

[36] "The Disvalue of Ontic Evil," p. 285.

[37] "Morality by Calculation of Values," p. 274

[38] On the other hand, the use of the term "evil" has been misunderstood as a condemnation by Janssens' of the goodness of creation. This is Quay's interpretation ("The Disvalue of Ontic Evil," p. 286). He suggests that this position "leads

sion say, of values, the mere natural structures of individual and social *bona* and *mala naturae* are not sufficient to tell us what we *ought* to do."[39] Exactly! He is correct in his assertion. This is precisely the point the revisionists, and with them Janssens, want to make. To decide which ontic goods to actualize, one must look at the values contained in them. This is not a facile task.

Conclusion

We have named and explicated the moral methodology of Louis Janssens. It is a method that is personalist and proportionalist, and therefore teleological. To say the first is to announce a turn to an historically conscious worldview, to take seriously the reality of time and space as they influence the existence and the destiny of human persons. It is to apply a new anthropology to moral theology. Heidegger spoke of the human person as *Dasein*, the Being-with-others, and Rahner affirmed the importance of the person in relationship to God through his/her existential reality. Janssens has applied and expanded these insights in a moral method.

Within this new anthropology we may speak both of what a person *is* and what a person *does*. First, let us examine what a person is. The shift in moral theology that Janssens represents is a movement away from the notion of "nature," a static concept about humanity, which has deontological roots. The term "nature" connotes an ideal, a template (located in the past, or deontologically) to which humankind must conform in his or her moral actions. Sometimes this ideal has been applied biologically

---

logically toward genuine dualism and collapse of faith in God's absolute goodness." Janssens' position is clear, however. Ontic evil is evil only in the sense that it imposes itself on humankind. E. coli is good; it lives peacefully in the digestive tract and helps with human digestion. When E. coli invades the human blood stream and causes infection, however, it becomes ontic evil, precisely because it has a negative effect on human life (cf. "Ontic Good and Evil: Premoral Values and Disvalues," pp. 61-62).

[39] "The Disvalue of Ontic Evil," p. 273.

(natural law physicalism) and put forth as a norm for human activity, as we saw above. Janssens, however, prefers to speak of "person," a term that takes seriously the role of human being as creature, co-creator, or at least a co-agent with God.[40] To say "person" is to embrace an open originality, a knowing and free reality, and all that this implies, that is, the nexus of relationships (with self, God, others, world). Fuchs says that the human being "is essentially person and has to understand himself therefore as a person—'in a human nature'—and achieve self-realization according to this self-understanding."[41]

It is interesting that Grisez sees this shift as affirming what he calls a "dualistic conception of the person."[42] If one attacks biologism, reasons Grisez, one separates the human being into body and spirit, thereby creating a dualism. This is not Janssens' intent. Rather, as we have seen, Janssens affirms the essential aspect of the bodily being of humanity as the vehicle through which the human person lives, grows and creates self. Janssens would deny, however, that bodily considerations are paramount in the evaluation of the human person adequately considered.

Further, to say "person" is to take seriously the role of history. Within human reality there is change. In his/her journey through time and space (history) the human person does not remain static. We can speak of this change on both the micro and macro level. On the micro level, the person who exists now is not completely congruent with the person who was several years ago. First, the individual person is an ever-growing reality, a self-creating entity in constant dialogue with self as s/he moves forward in time and space in the process of actuating self. Who I am points me toward who I shall become: who I am becoming contributes to who I am, as I become. Not only have I changed physically (albeit with some regret and struggling acceptance), but the

---

[40] I borrow the terms from Kelly, p. 436.

[41] "The Absoluteness of Moral Terms," p. 108. Fuchs seems to have been influenced somewhat by Janssens' thinking here, in that he cites both *Personne et société* and *Personalisme en democratisering*.

[42] Ibid., p. 204, n. 43.

complex of values, goals, ideas, and so forth, which comprise the "spiritual" me, are different from what they were in my past. The "spiritual me" is the product of my action through the "physical me," the *esprit incarné*.

There is a macro dimension as well. An example will illustrate what I mean. Humanity of the age of Abraham—accepting of human sacrifice and slavery, for instance—is not the humanity of the twentieth century. As the human community has travelled through its own history, it has discovered new human-worthy values which have become a part of its deposit of culture. Humanity no longer tolerates child sacrifice nor the subjugation of other human persons against their wills. On the macro level the person is related to the sum of persons who, *qua* persons, are in the same process as is the individual person. The dialogue between the growing individual and the growing corporate person is the dialogue between the subjective and objective culture to which Janssens refers. It may prove helpful to diagram the various dynamic relationships that are implied here. We can speak of the dynamics of act, of person, of persons in the collective sense, and of the relationship between the individual person and the collectivity of persons (society).

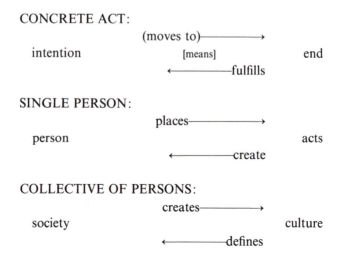

CONCRETE ACT:

                      (moves to)————→

intention   [means]   end

                   ←————————fulfills

SINGLE PERSON:

                      places————————→

person   acts

                   ←————————create

COLLECTIVE OF PERSONS:

                    creates————————→

society   culture

                   ←————————defines

CULTURE:

$$\text{provides} \longrightarrow$$

subjective culture   objective culture

$$\longleftarrow \text{provides}$$

The human person, in Janssens' method, is the image of God in historical, temporal context, that is, as an open, limited being. To use classical terms, the human person is called to actuate his/her potency as individual and as group in his/her various relationships.

Second, the new anthropology is occupied with what a person does. This activity is implied by the diagrams above. The task of the human person, says Janssens, is to create him/herself, that is, through free and conscious acts to fulfill his or her destiny. The goal or model for this task is the human person adequately considered. The human person stands out *before* each moral act as the criterion for determining it, the value which it seeks most fully to embody in good. This model functions normatively, as Janssens says so frequently, for the assessment of human action. It is the objective (and in some sense, as we noted in chapter three, deontologic) component of the moral act. This notion of relationships is key, since it locates the human person in what I shall call a pre-context. The content of this pre-context is available for the person in his/her moral decison making, that is, for the project of self-actualization. What I mean by this is that the human person is given a nexus of relationships (objective culture: models of how a human being can/should be, embodied in values, norms, etc.), as we noted above, which provide objective criteria of what is morally right. As this pre-context is internalized, it becomes the content of what the moral person is. It is the pre-context for moral action. The good *embodied* is for each person the good that he or she is. That is, it is less the external act considered as moral, but the person considered as moral that is important.

What a person does forms what I shall call a post-context. Each human act contributes in turn to the reality of what that person (subjective culture) is and to the total reality of persons (objective culture). The resultant reality can be evaluated over against the totality of the objective culture (values, etc.) in order to judge its moral adequacy. It then becomes part of a *new* pre-context for the individual and for the group in the assessment of new moral dilemmas. How valid this new pre-context is depends on the care with which it has been chosen, that is, on the attention which the concrete agent(s) paid to the objective criteria in assessing his/her (their) moral decision making. Sufficient care—assuming the optimistic view of human person that Janssens does—results in "good" results, that is, acceptable criteria for future judgments.

Ultimately the methodology of Louis Janssens is a methodology of the tensions and of the dialogue diagramed above. It is through a dynamic reciprocity that what is possible for persons and society becomes real. It is on the journey through time and space that humanity moves toward and eventually meets its destiny. This is not a static model but a personal historically-conscious model, which changes. Thus, Janssens' method is inductive, gleaning its data from the ongoing process of living life in its historical context. It is born in human experience, which in turn begets the model for human activity. The self-creating human person is also self-defining.

As we noted above, however, we are in no danger of dropping into the abyss of subjectivism—Janssens never does. The process of self-creating/self-defining is always situated. That is precisely what the diagrams above show. The person, or as a collective, persons, are always in touch and responsible to the objective criteria. The human person is never "adequately considered" outside the sphere of these criteria. The internal activity of persons must always attend to and embrace the external components. Activity is then evaluated in light of them.

We have said that Janssens' method is proportionalist. The proportionalist seeks as his/her end the good, that is the good of the human person. Each action must, insofar as possible, achieve this end. The proportionalist takes seriously both the responsibility of human decision making in the task of self-realization and the existence of evil. Janssens' moral method illustrates both. His clear insight into the distinction between ontic and moral evil demonstrates this. It stands as perhaps his most significant contribution to Roman Catholic moral method.

Recognizing the value of ecclesial tradition by meticulous attention to the insights of Thomas Aquinas and their application in a modern moral context, Janssens takes the bold experiment we call creation seriously. God has imaged humanity in freedom and in knowledge, fashioning others like himself and setting them as incarnate spirits within the relationships of reality. And "God blessed them.... God looked at everything he had made and found it very good" (Gen 1: 28-31). The task of this wondrous creature—woman and man—is to become more and more the image of the One who shaped him/her in the divine image and likeness (Gen 1:26), to discover in a deeper and deeper way the meaning of him/herself. And, as Joseph Selling has aptly stated: "If you find the human person adequately considered, you will understand the meaning of good and evil, and if you do that, you will be *prepared* to *begin* a moral discussion. For if you do it disinterestedly, you will find the core of the major insights of Janssens' work...."[43] We trust we have begun this quest. As we stand on the shoulders of the likes of Aquinas and Heidegger, Rahner and Blondel, in the company of Louis Janssens, we look forward to the horizon of our destiny. With Janssens we can repeat the words of Blondel he quotes so often in his writings: *Nous sommes embarqués.*

---

[43] Joseph Selling, letter October 11, 1987.

Academic Bibliography of Louis Janssens

"De leer van Sint Gregorius van Nyssa over de eucharistie." *Algemeen Nederlands Eucharistisch Tijdschrift* 15 (1936) 65-71. (Under the name of O. Van Der Bergen).

"La filiation divine par grâce d'après saint Cyrille d'Alexandrie." Ph.D. dissertation, University of Louvain, 1937.

"Notre filiation divine d'après saint Cyrille d'Alexandrie." *Ephemerides theologicae lovanienses* 15 (1938) 233-278; *Sylloge excerptorum* 5 (1938): fasc. 1.

Personne et société: théories actuelles et essai doctrinal. Dissertationes ad gradum magistri in Facultate Theologica vel in Facultate Iuris Canonici consequendum conscriptae, series II -Tomus 32. Gembloux: Duculot, 1939.

"Vrees en geweld (De menselijke handeling)," in *Geestelijke voordrachten der Geloofsverdediging.* Vol. V, 1939-40. Antwerp: Geloofsverdediging, 1940.

Het sacramentele huwelijk. Antwerp: Geloofsverdediging, 1940.

"Wat richt de activiteit der enkelingen in het sociale leven?" *Streven* 8 (1940-41) 63-72.

Problemen van kerk en staat. Mechlin: St. Franciscus, 1941.

Ons heilig misoffer. Louvain: Vlaamse Drukkerij, 1942.

Foreword to *De ethiek van den arbeid*, by Nabor Devolder. Economischsociale bibliotheek. Monographien, 20. Antwerp, 1942.

"Het communisme." *Verslagboek der academische sociale studiedagen.* Given at Louvain 26 to 28 October. Antwerp: 't Groeit, 1945.

God en de mensch. Leuven: Davidsfonds, 1946.

"Het geestelijke en het tijdelijke." *Ons Geloof* 28 (1946) 237-247.

"Cultuur en Christendom." *Onze Alma Mater* 1 (1947/3) 11-14.

"Streven naar waarheid als kenmerk van een universitaire vorming." In *Vorming aan de Universiteit* (Uitgaven van het universitaire centrum voor Meisjesstudenten.) Louvain: Nauwelaerts, 1947. Pp. 51-64.

"Trouw aan de kerk." *Ons Geloof* 29 (1947) 3-14.

"Vox temporis, vox Dei." *Ons Geloof* 29 (1947) 193-214.

"Tijd en ruimte in de moraal." In *Miscellanea moralia in honorem eximii Domini Arthur Janssen.* Bibliotheca Ephemeridum Theologicarum Lovaniensium, 2. Louvain, 1947. Pp. 181-197.

"Daden met meerdere gevolgen." *Collectanea Mechliniensia* 17 (1947) 621-633.

"Het pluralisme: de verschillende stromingen." In *Het pluralisme en actuele problemen. Verslagboek van de XXXIe Vlaamse sociale week te Leuven.* Brussels: A.C.W., 1949. Pp. 19-32.

"Sociale geneeskunde." *Streven* 17 (1949-50) 617-626.

"De sanering van de repressie." *Kultuurleven* 17 (1950) 332-346.

"De taak van de Staat." In *De christelijke sociale leer en de hedendaagse gemeenschap. Verslagboek van de XXXIIe Vlaamse sociale week te Leuven.* Brussels: A.C.W., 1950. Pp. 95-110.

"Liefde en sociaal leven." Radio-causeries, April 1951. Antwerp-Bilthoven: 't Groeit, 1951.

"Cultuur, een gave voor allen." *K.W.B. Leiding.* June 1951, pp. 20-24; July 1971, pp. 21-24.

"Coördinatie der medico-sociale werken." *Leiding* 4 (1951) 99-112.

Coördination des œuvres médico-sociales. Gent: Vanmelle, 1951.

"Vrijheid en algemeen welzijn." In *De vrijheid in de huidige samenleving. Verslagboek van de XXXIIIe Vlaamse sociale week te Leuven.* Brussels: A.C.W., 1951. Pp. 67-82.

"De betekenis van de christelijke naastenliefde in onze tijd." *Pastor Bonus* 29 (1952) 2-8.

"Gelijkheid en ongelijkheid." In *Het blijvende en het wisselende in de maatschappelijke verhoudingen. Verslagboek van de 21e Limburgse sociale studieweek.* Rolduc, 1952. Pp. 108-124.

"Pauselijke uitspraken over de periodieke onthouding in het huwelijk." *Pastor Bonus* 29 (1952) 131-135.

"Naastenliefde en rechtvaardigheid." *Kultuurleven* 19 (1952) 9-18.

"Orientation de la médecine et de l'assurance maladie." *Orientation mutualiste* 5 (1952) 113-126.

"De rechten van de mens." *Tijdschrift voor politiek* 2 (1952) 523-550.

"Huidige huwelijksproblemen." *Collectanea Mechliniensia* 37 (1952) 221-234; 337-348.

"Eigendomsproblemen." *Politicia-Berichten* 2 (1953) 3-13.

Morale et problèmes démographiques. Etudes morales, sociales, et juridiques. Louvain: Desbarax, 1953.

Het kaderpersoneel en zijn sociale verantwoordelijkheid de arbeidsgemeenschap. Antwerp: L.B.C., 1953.

"Christelijke eigendomsleer." *Pastor Bonus* 30 (1953) 199-213.

"Moraal en wereldbevolking." *Streven* 21 (1953-54) 97-107; 237-245.

"De unie van Mechelen en het medebeheer." *Politicia-Berichten* 4 (1954) 1-8.

"Les bases du personnalisme." *Service social dans le monde* 13 (1954) 50-54.

"Gij, Priester, en de leek." *Pastor Bonus* 31 (1953) 2-20.

Droits personnels et autorité. Louvain: Nauwelaerts, 1954.

La protection de la famille ouvrière. Kortrijk: Vooruitgang, 1954.

"Staking en moraal." In *Verslagboek van de XXXV Vlaamse sociale week te Leuven*. Louvain, 1954.

Staking en moraal. Brussels: A.C.W., 1954.

Grève et morale. Brussels: C.S.C., 1954.

"Gezag en onderneming." *De gids op maatschappelijk gebied* 45 (1954) 329-345.

"Autorité et entreprise." *Les dossiers de l'action sociale catholique* 31 (1954) 401-417.

"Het christendom, godsdienst van de Drieëenheid of van de liefde?" *Pastor Bonus* 31 (1954) 196-202.

"De katholieke leek en de politiek." *Tijdschrift voor politiek* 4 (1954) 408-421.

"De taak van de huidige staat." *Politica-Berichten* 5 (1955) 1-19.

"The Task of Today's State." *American College Bulletin* 34 (1955) 33-47.

"Het gezag van de ouders." *De gids op maatschappelijk gebied* 46 (1955) 269-285.

"Participaciòn de los pueblos en los bienes econòmicos." *Archivode Migraciòn* 1 (1955) 23-25.

"Philosophie sociale." *Service social dans le monde* 14 (1955) 49-51.

"Vijf en twintig jaar encycliek: *Divini Illius Magistri.*" *Vlaams opvoedkundig tijdschrift* 35 (1955) 63-67.

"Huwelijkstheologie." *Huwelijk en gezen*. Special nummer van *Universitas* 16 (1954-55) 81-123.

"Moderne situatie-ethiek in het licht van de klassieke leer over het geweten." *Tijdschrift voor zielkunde en opvoedingsleer* 21 (1956) 172-198; *Pastor Bonus* 33 (1956) 71-87.

"Het meisje en de universiteit." *Universitas* 17 (1955-56) 117-127.

"De norm van de zedelijkheid en de integriteit van de persoon." *Collectanea Mechliniensia* 26 (1956) 161-186.

"De kristelijke zin van het lijden." *Hospitalia* 1 (1956) 3-9.

"Le sens chrétien de la souffrance." *Hospitalia* 1 (1956/3) 3-8.

"Sinn und Wert der Herz-Jesu-Andacht für die Zeitseelsorge. *Anima* 11 (1956) 198-210.

"Recht en moraal." *Sint-Lucasblad* 28 (1956) 521-534.

"Ben ik de bewaker van mijn broeder?" *Palfijn* 16 (1956) 53-56.

Personalisme en democratisering. Brussels: Arbeiderspers, 1957, 1965.

"Vrije keuze en verantwoordelijkheid van het geneeskundig korps." *Sint-Lucasblad* 29 (1957) 375-388.

"Ethiek en onderneming." *Politica* 8 (1958) 1-21.

"De geneeskunde als vrij beroep." *De gids op maatschappelijk gebied* 49 (1958) 123-144.

"Comment le coopérateur répond aux besoins de notre temps." *Brochure du congres central de Don Bosco.* June 1958. Woluwe-Saint-Pierre: Centrale Don Bosco, 1958.

"L'inhibition de l'ovulation est-elle moralement licite?" *Ephemerides theologicae lovanienses* 34 (1958) 357-360.

"Ist die Reglung der Ovulation sittlich erlaubt?" *Theologische Digest* 1 (1958) 248-251.

"Christendom en geweten." *De gids op maatschappelijk gebied* 4 (1958) 891-908.

"The Rights of the Person." *American College Bulletin* 38 (1959) 12-15; 113-121.

"De theologie van het huwelijk." In *Huwelijk en gezin*. Universitaschrift, 5. 3rd edition. Louvain: Universitas, 1959. Pp. 89-153.

"Justice à l'échelle de l'humanité." *Justice dans le monde* 1 (1959-1960) 17-35.

"World Justice." *World Justice* 1 (1959-60) 15-34.

"Het huwelijk als opdracht tot heiligheid." (nota's bij een conferentie-schema). Uitgaven van het Centrum voor godsdienstige bezinning. Louvain, 1960.

"Problemen rond de periodieke onthouding." *Huwelijk en huisgezin* 26 (1960) 20-31.

"Liefde in heilige tekens." *Huwelijk en huisgezin* 26 (1960) 37-42.

"Echtelijke liefde en kuisheid." *Huwelijk en huisgezin* 26 (1960) 62-68.

"Tucht en ontucht." *Huwelijk en huisgezin* 26 (1960) 100-106.

"De heilige band." *Huwelijk en huisgezin* 26 (1960) 109-114.

"Wet en geweten." *Huwelijk en huisgezin* 26 (1960) 132-139.

"Ervaren we onze kristelijke huwelijksliefde?." *Huwelijk en huisgezin* 26 (1960) 145-149.

"Liefde en lijden." *Huwelijk en huisgezin* 26 (1960) 181-187.

"De inhoud van de rechtvaardigheid wordt steeds rijker." *De gids op maatschappelijk gebied* 51 (1960) 121-140.

"Morele en juridische aspecten bij de transplantatie." *Transplantatie* (Symposium voor de studenten van de medische faculteit der R.K. Universiteit Nijmegen), 1961. Pp. 149-155.

Mater et magistra: voor een beter inzicht in de sociale encycliek van Paus Johannes XXIII. 15 May 1961.

"*Mater et Magistra.*" *Vita-documentatie* 3 (1962/63) 3-12.

"Doden uit medelijden." *Pastor Bonus* 39 (1962) 544-548.

"Humanisme en personalisme." *Dietsche Warande en Belfort* 107 (1962) 707-724.

"Het moreel standpunt tegenover de kalmeermiddelen." (summary) *Geesteshygiëne*, 1963/3. Pp. 38-39.

Uw grotere kinderen en de liefde. Leuven: Boerinnenbond, 1963.

"Morale conjugale et progestogènes." *Ephemerides theologicae lova-*

nienses 39 (1963) 787-826; J. Ferin et L. Janssens. "Progestogenes et morale conjugale." Bibliotheca Ephemeridum Theologicarum Lovaniensium, 22. Leuven-Gembloux: Duculot, 1963. Pp. 9-48.

Foreword to *Het probleem van de ontwikkelingslanden: proeve van een morele stellingname*, by Leonard Van Baelen. De christen in de tijd, 15. Antwerp: Patmos, 1963; *Morale du developpement, le probleme des pays en voie de developpement*. Lyon: Mappus, 1968.

Foreword to *Gemoedsleven en deugd: Thomas contra Suarez?*, by Christiaan Paul Sporken. Nijmegen-Utrecht: Dekker en van de Vegt, 1963.

"Met de andersdenkenden in een gemeenschappelijke wereld." *De gids op maatschappelijk gebied* 51 (1963) 287-307.

"Régulation des naissances et collaboration des catholiques avec les non-catholiques." *Justice dans le monde* 5 (1963-64) 22-42.

"Catholics and non-Catholics: Their Collaboration on Family Planning." *World Justice* 5 (1963-64) 21-40.

"Moraal en genesskunde." *De Gazet* (Antwerp), 19-23, 26 February 1964.

Liberté de conscience et liberté religieuse. Paris-Bruges: Desclée de Brouwer, 1964.

Libertad de consciencia y religiosa. Concilio Ecumenico Vaticano II, 7. Buenos Aires: Guadalupe, 1964.

Freedom of Conscience and Religious Freedom. Translated by Brother Lorenzo. Staten Island: Alba, 1966.

"The Foundation for Freedom of Conscience." *American College Bulletin* 43 (1964) 16-21.

"Godsdienstvrijheid." In *Naar een vernieuwde Kerk*. Edited by J. D'Hoogh. Leuven: Davidsfonds, 1965. Pp. 103-123.

"Le respect de la vie au regard de la conscience chrétienne." In *Peut-on tuer? Des personnalités éminentes d'une dizaine de pays répondent: la vie est sacrée*. Bruges: Desclée De Brouwer, 1965. Pp. 95-98.

"Morele problemen in verband met geboortespreiding." *Leuven geneeskundig tijdschrift*, 1965. Pp. 171-192.

"Moral Problems Involved in Responsible Parenthood." *One in Christ* 1 (1965): 243-260; *Louvain Studies* 1 (1966-67) 3-18.

Echtelijke liefde en verantwoord ouderschap. Kasterlee: De Vroente, 1966.

"Chasteté conjugale selon l'encyclique *Casti Connubii* et suivant la constitution pastorale *Gaudium et Spes*." *Ephemerides theologicae lovanienses* 42 (1966) 513-554.

"Geweten en zedelijke waarde." *Collationes Brugenses et Gandavenses* 12 (1966): 433-455; 13 (1967) 33-44.

"Historicity in Conjugal Morality: Evolution and Continuity." *Louvain Studies* 1 (1966-67) 262-268.

"Les grandes étapes de la morale chrétienne du mariage." In *Aux sources de la morale conjugale*. Réponses chrétiennes. Gembloux: Duculot-Paris: Lethielleux, 1967. Pp. 125-155.

Mariage et fécondité, De Casti Connubii à Gaudium et Spes. Réponses chrétiennes. Gembloux: Duculot-Paris: Lethielleux, 1967.

"Conciliaire verklaring over de godsdienstvrijheid." *De gids op maatschappelijk gebied* 59 (1968) 759-779.

"Over de encycliek *Humanae Vitae*: zin van huwelijks en gezinsleven." Middelen tot geboortespreiding. *Kana* 44 (1968) 2-9.

"Na *Humanae Vitae*." *Collectanea Mechliniensia*. 53 (1968) 421-449.

"Considerations on *Humanae Vitae*." *Louvain Studies* 2 (1968-69) 231-253.

"Leergezag en moraal; een kernpunt in de discussie *Humanae Vitae*," with L. Geysels. *De nieuwe boodschap* 96 (1969) 74-83.

"Christus en de moraal." *Christendom en secularisatie*. Antwerpse Theologische Studieweek 1969. Antwerp: Patmos, 1970. Pp. 66-82.

"Personalist Morals." *Louvain Studies* 3 (1970-71) 5-16.

"Het christeliljke in de ethiek." *Sacerdos* 38 (1971) 385-398; *De Weg* (Antwerp), 6 (1971) 33-44.

"Ontic Evil and Moral Evil." Louvain Studies 4 (1972-73) 115-156; *Readings in Moral Theology 1: Moral Norms and Catholic Tradition*. Edited by Charles E. Curran and Richard A. McCormick. New York: Paulist Press, 1979. Pp. 40-93.

Christelijk leven met een autonome moraal. Studieweek Haasrode. 20-24 August 1973.

De inhoud van de rechtvaardigheid wordt steeds rijker. Godsdienstig jaarprogramma 1973-74. Boerenbond.

"De zedelijke normen." In *Ethische vragen voor onze tijd: hulde aan Mgr. Victor Heylen*. Antwerp: De Nederlandse Boekhandel, 1977. Pp. 37-58.

"Ontstaan en groei van de morele normen in betrekking tot de seksualiteit." In *Opvoeding tot relatiebekwaamheid. Verslagboek van de Vlieberg-Sencie-Leergang Afdeling Cathechese 1976*. Antwerp-Amsterdam: Patmos, 1977. Pp. 83-98.

"Norms and Priorities in a Love Ethics." *Louvain Studies* 6 (1976-77) 207-238.

"Louisa Brown en de ethiek." *De Standaard*, 8 September 1978.

"Normen en prioriteiten in een ethiek van de liefde." *Sacerdos* 46 (1978-79) 15-31; 129-150.

Waarheen met huwelijk en gezin? C.M.B.V., 1979.

"Morele verantwoordelijkheid in het verkeer." *Davidsfonds mededelingen* 12 (1979/4): 11-13.

"Kunstmatige inseminatie: ethische beschouwingen." *Verpleegkundige en gemeenschapszorg* 35 (1979) 220-244.

"Ethische beschouwingen." In *Bespreekbaarheid van ethische problematiek in ons christelijk zienkenhuis*. Caritas Dienst Vlaams-Brabant/Mechlin, 26 February 1980.

"Artificial Insemination: Ethical Considerations." *Louvain Studies* 8 (1980-81) 3-29.

"De morele ontwikkeling volgens Lawrence Kohlberg." *Collationes* 10 (1980) 258-295.

"Over geboorteregeling (Info 83)." *Mensen onderweg* 83 (1981/1).

"Waarheen met de moraal?" *Naar een nieuwe levenshouding?*, Brussels: National Secretariaat K.G.B., 1982.

"Saint Thomas Aquinas and the Question of Proportionality." *Louvain Studies* 9 (1982-83) 26-46.

"Transplantation d'organes." *La foi et le temps* 13 (1983) 318-324.

Foreward to *The 1980 Synod of Bishops On the Role of the Family. An Exposition of the Event and an Analysis of its Texts*, by Jan Grootaers and Joseph A. Selling. BETL, 64. Louvain: University Press-Peeters, 1983.

"Evoluerende moraal in verband met homoseksualiteit." *Kultuurleven* 51 (1984) 147-166.

"Personalisme en proportionaliteit." *Leven, lijden en sterven*, Algemene Kliniek Sint-Jan Brussels (1984).

"Gewetensvorming." In *God is groter: Werkboek rond het geloven*, edited by Joris Baers and Ernest Henau. 3rd edition: Lannoo, Tielt-Weesp, 1985. Pp. 452-459.

"De moraal in stroomversnelling." *De Bazuin* 68 (18 October 1985) 3, 8.

"Personalisme en Seksualiteit." In *Jeugd en sesualiteit*. Bijdragen tot de jeugdpastoraal, 2. Louvain: Acco, 1985.

"Perspectives and Implications of Some Arguments of Saint Thomas," speech, 6 March 1987, Louvain, Belgium; also published as "A Moral Understanding of Some Arguments of Saint Thomas." *Ephemerides theologicae lovanienses* 63 (1987) 354-360.

"Ontic Good and Evil: Premoral Values and Disvalues." *Louvain Studies* 12 (1987) 62-82.

"Verantwoord ouderschap en methoden van geboortenregeling in het licht van het geloofsboek'." *Sacerdos* 55 (1988) 145-155.

"Time and Space in Morals." In *Personalist Morals*. Translated by Jan Jans. Edited by Joseph A. Selling. Leuven: University Press, 1988. Pp. 9-22.

"The Non-infallible Magisterium and Theologians," *Louvain Studies* 14 (1989) 195-259.

INDEX OF NAMES

SUBJECT INDEX